Adolf Hitler Biography

A Comprehensive Biography of One of the Most Feared Leaders of the 20th Century- From Gefreiter to Führer

Author: Nichola Wil

Nichola Wil

Free Gift

This book includes a bonus booklet. This giveaway may be for a limited time only. All information on how you can secure your gift right now can be found at the end of this book.

Table of Contents

These 14 New Habits Will Double Your Income, from Today

An Easy Cheat Sheet to Adopting 14 Powerful Success Habits:

Stop Procrastinating and Start Earning with Intent Now!

Are Your Bad Habits Keeping You from the Life You Want?

Mine definitely were, but then I dedicated myself to *new habits* – and everything changed!

Most people get stuck in same old routines. We eat the same breakfast, we talk to the same people. Human beings are creatures of habit, and it locks us into negative cycles we don't even know are there. Like me, you've had enough of the same-old, same-old. It's time for change!

This guide gives you the 14 most high impact habits that helped me double my income nearly instantly, when I set out on this journey. I will help you change, and I'll make it stick!

This FREE Cheat Sheet contains:

- Daily success habits that the most successful people in the world live by

- Common, but little-known habits that will surprise you

- Details on what Stephen Covey, Oprah Winfrey, Elon Musk, Bill Gates and Albert Einstein did that you aren't doing to maximize your earning potential

- Tips on how to overcome habit fatigue

- The reality of adopting difficult, challenging habits and the rewards that result

Scroll below and click the link to claim **your cheat sheet!**

It's tough to admit that you're doing it wrong. I went through it, and it sucks. After that I was free to change however necessary, to meet my goals. I want you to know that change is waiting for you. This guide is so easy to follow, and if you put it to work in your life – you will double your income.

Adopt these habits, and change your life.

CLICK HERE!!

Book Description:

Are you interested in learning more about Adolf Hitler, one of the most feared leaders of all time? In this candid guide, you'll discover what made the boy such a successfully murderous man.

Adolf Hitler. This name triggers a range of emotions for so many people. Hatred. Fear. Fascination. Historians have been studying his story since he died at the end of World War 2. What drove a young man from Austria to seek out power, and use it to murder so many innocent people?

In *Hitler's Biography*, I'll take you through the early beginnings of Hitler's childhood, right up until that fateful day when he shot himself in a bunker after the 3rd Reich failed – and he had changed the world forever. A darker time in history we've not yet seen. This is his story.

In this biography you'll discover:

- Where Hitler came from and what inspired him to extremist beliefs

- His role in creating a new ideology, one that persists today

- The young, ambitious politician and how he rose to prominence

- How the Führer came to be, and how he gathered his power

- Hitler's final solution, and the devastation it created

- How Hitler was beaten, and his final days

By studying the past, we prepare for a brighter future. Learn about the life of a man who made such a significant impact on history, and the world – and an entire generation of people.

True evil rises when conditions are desperate enough. Enjoy the story of a dictator who rose, and was later toppled by a world that refused to let evil win.

Explore the life of Adolf Hitler in this book.

Get it now and learn how it happened!

Introduction

It is said that "The sleep of reasons produces monsters" and this quote seems to be very appropriate for the twentieth century, a period in which economic hardships and crisis led to massive conflicts like World War I and World War II. These periods are favorable for the development of radical movements because when large masses of people are suffering from poverty, unemployment, and other social calamities, extremist movements are developing and in some cases, they can seize power in such affected countries. The end of World War I was the period for dramatic changes, as historic empires which stood for centuries collapsed under the pressure of the very ethnic groups which used to form these empires. The Russian Empire was destroyed by the rise of Bolshevism, while the Austrian Empire collapsed, and eleven other nations emerged from its ashes. It seemed that the German ethnics had the most to suffer because the end of the war brought severe sanctions upon them and some of them were integrated into other countries like Poland or Czechoslovakia. The German people were in search for a leader to amend the wrongs which were done to them by the Allies and to punish the people who betrayed them and signed the ceasefire armistice and the Treaty of Versailles. As it happened, this leader that they were looking for was not even a German citizen. In fact, he was an Austrian who moved to Bavaria (Munich).

Adolf Hitler was a character who emerged from a chaotic and weakened Germany, and many Germans thought he would be the savior who would take the country out of ruin and guide it to glory and greatness. Growing up in a time of social turmoil and being exposed to anti-Semitic and racist rhetoric, he accumulated a lot of hatred towards Jews and other Slavic nations. As he was an Austrian citizen, he felt ashamed of being a part of a multi-ethnic state, in which the German ethnics were disadvantaged compared to the Slavic ethnics and even the Jews. He despised the Austrian social policy and came to hate Vienna for its multi-ethnicity. As the period he spent in Vienna was marked by starvation and poverty, he still followed an artist's way of life and did nothing to change his social status and also to get a reliable income. He was just a dreamer, very passionate about German culture and Wagner's operas, which would shape his beliefs of German ultranationalism.

Vienna was never a place which he could call home, but he saw Munich as a place to which he belonged, a true German city. It was here where he put to personal use his oratorical talents. He became the voice of a small right-wing party, with nationalist, anti-Marxist, and anti-Semitic beliefs. His message started to reach bigger crowds as his speeches made sense to bigger audiences. He became the most important figure of the Nazi party, as he imposed his visions on the other members. The Beer Hall Putsch was a setback for his political career, but it gave him the perfect opportunity to reflect and think of better ways to seize power. During the time he spent in prison, he compiled his ideas and beliefs into a book which served as a political manifesto for the Nazi party. After his release, he built the party making it stronger than ever and waited for the right opportunity to seize power. As some would say, Hitler used democracy to kill democracy itself, meaning that he had risen to power in democratic ways and once he was in power he declared himself the Führer, concentrating the whole power into his hands. The German people came to respect, love, and fear him, as they could see the power of Germany increasing and the country restored to its former glory. However, too much power also attracted enemies, within or outside Germany, but also it increased his ego, as he was the person responsible for the German Army defeats on the battlefield. The defeats were too severe to recover from them, and the allied forces were recovering the territory occupied by the Germans.

Everything comes to an end, and Hitler's dreams and ambitions were destroyed and completely shattered in the ruins of Berlin. In a century with great political figures like Churchill and Roosevelt, Hitler is considered to be the biggest negative figure of this period (and probably in the whole history of humankind) because he can be considered responsible for the deaths of more than twenty million lives, civilian and soldiers.

This book comes with a FREE Bonus chapter section as a gift. You can download them for free. The free content can be found at the bottom of this book.

Chapter 1
Hitler's Childhood and Youth

"I can recall the gaunt, pale-faced youth pretty well. He had definite talent, though in a narrow field. But he lacked self-discipline, being notoriously cantankerous, willful, arrogant and bad-tempered. He faced some difficulty in fitting in at school. Moreover, he was lazy…his enthusiasm for hard work evaporated all too quickly. He reacted with ill-concealed hostility to advice or reproof; at the same time he demanded of his fellow pupils their unqualified subservience, fancying himself in the role of leader…"

– Dr. Eduard Hümer, one of Hitler's teachers.

Hitler's Origins

There were many theories related to Hitler's origins, some of the historians claiming that the feared Nazi leader had Jewish origins. Such a theory was never proven, but there is still a mystery about the origin of Hitler's father, Alois Hitler Sr. He was the illegitimate son of Maria Anna Schicklgruber and was born in 1837. At this point, Alois was recognized as a Schicklgruber. However, in 1842, Alois's mother married Johann Georg Hiedler, and he became Alois's father, a person who was registered as Georg Hitler. The Schicklgrubers were a humble family, simple and poor peasants from the North-Western part of Lower Austria.

Alois was the first ambitious person in the family, a person who wanted to climb up the social ladder. At an early age, he was employed in a modest position at the Austrian Ministry of Finance, but despite his background and poor education, he managed to get promoted to higher positions. Therefore, he obtained a supervisor status in 1861, then a customs service position in 1864. In 1870 he gained a customs officer position and then moved to Braunau am Inn the next year, where he became a customs inspector in 1875. Being a social climber, he may have embraced the name of Hitler, instead of Schicklgruber, because it was simple and appealing, and starting with the Final Authorization of 1877 he always signed Alois Hitler. Alois met his future wife (Klara Pölzl) long before having an impressive career. In fact, after the name change, they were practically second cousins. Klara Pölzl was the eldest surviving daughter of Johanna Hüttler with Johann Baptist Pölzl, a smallholder from Spital. However, it was Klara's grandfather, Johann Nepomuk Hüttler, the brother of Johann Georg Hiedler, who adopted Alois after this brother passed away. This is how their family connection can be explained. When Klara was sixteen, she moved from the farm her family owned in Spital to work as a maid in the house of Alois Hitler from Braunau am Inn.

Although he had a remarkable career, the personal affairs of Alois were not in order. He married three times. The first time to a woman older than himself called Anna Glasserl, but the marriage ended in 1880. The second time, he married a very young woman, Franziska Matzelberger, but she died of tuberculosis at the age of twenty-three. By the time his second wife died in August 1884, Alois had nine children, but four of them died during infancy. During his two marriages, Klara was no longer a maid in Alois's household, but when Franziska was sick, she had been relocated for fresh air in the surroundings of Braunau am Inn. The children from the last marriage were very small, so Alois turned to Klara to take care of his young children. Soon after Franziska was buried, Klara became pregnant, but a marriage between two second cousins was not possible, so they needed to get the Church's approval. As the condition of Klara was becoming more obvious, the approval from the Church arrived at the end of 1884. Alois Hitler and Klara Pölzl officially married on January 7, 1885. The first children of their marriage died very young, only living up to two or three years. The first child who was named Gustav was born in May 1885 and died in December 1887. The second child was Ida, who just like Gustav had diphtheria and died in January 1888. The third child was Otto, who died within a few days following his birth.

On April 20, 1889, at around 6:30 pm, Adolf Hitler was born. It was the Saturday before Easter when the fourth child of Alois and Klara Hitler came into this world. Also, he was the first one of this marriage who didn't die in the early years. Besides his previous brothers and sisters, from his father's first and second marriages, Adolf had another brother called Edmund (born in 1894 and died in 1900) and a sister Paula, who was born in 1896. Alois had a very good income which was able to assure a very comfortable middle-class life for the Hitler family. However, this didn't mean that the Hitlers had a permanent residency in the Braunau am Inn town. In the autumn of 1898, Alois bought a house with a piece of land in Leonding, a village just outside Linz, probably for better education of the children. Linz was always regarded by Adolf Hitler as his home town, and he always thought of it as the most "Germanic" town of the Austro-Hungarian Empire, which united eleven different nationalities in the same state. It was a nice place to grow up, as little Adolf enjoyed a childhood without any worries, but the carefree life was about to end.

Studies and Passions

After the death of his brother Edmund in 1900 and because his elder brother Alois junior was already living a rebellious life far away from home, Alois senior's ambitions fell on Adolf's shoulders. Therefore, he wanted Adolf to attain Realschule, a school which emphasized modern subjects like technical studies and science, which can be a very good starting point for higher education. He despised the humanistic studies and considered them very impractical for career development. By the time Alois noticed that his son Adolf was showing too much interest in drawing, he wanted to avert him from the humanistic studies and the lifestyle which comes with it.

Secondary school was a nightmare for Adolf Hitler, as he didn't have much time to develop relationships to make friends. He had to commute each day from Leonding to Linz and back, a journey which took more than an hour of his day. He despised most of the classes, so his school performance was poor and mediocre. Certainly, not something his father was dreaming of. At this point, he had already become an introvert and an antisocial teenager. The relationship he had with his father was also difficult, going to Realschule being the starting point of conflict between Adolf and his father. This was also the period in which he took refuge in the stories of heroism from the German past and became a fanatic German nationalist, with hate and contempt of the Austrian Empire. In his primary school days, Adolf was just like most of the children, happy and playful. However, during secondary school, he turned into a rebellious and stubborn teenager who apparently had no purpose in life. He had become everything his father stood against and rejected.

Alois Hitler died on January 3, 1903, leaving to his family more than a comfortable situation. This meant that young Adolf was free to follow his dream and nobody could influence his goals. He continued to have poor results at school and tried to convince his mother to abandon this school. In 1905, the family moved to Linz, but Adolf left the Realschule in the same year. He enjoyed the carefree life again, with no goals, with his mother, his aunt, Johanna and his little sister, Paula looking after his needs. Adolf was free to pursue the lifestyle of an artist, and most of his activities were related to painting or writing poetry. He fantasized about becoming a great artist, and he even took piano lessons in his attempt to become a musician. Going to the Linz Opera was one of his favorite activities, as he realized that becoming an artist means socializing with other art lovers. It was at the opera that he familiarized himself with the work of Richard Wagner, as these dramas presented tales from a glorious and mythical Germanic past. He fell in love irremediably with the work of Wagner, which would lay the foundation to a new ideology.

His love of the arts made him persuade his mother to finance his trip to Vienna to study the pictures from the Court Museum. He wandered for two weeks as a tourist in the Austrian capital, sightseeing the most important tourist attractions. It was during this trip that he formed the idea of attending the Viennese Academy of Fine Arts. His aunt, Johanna even made a loan to finance young Adolf's studies at the finest art school in the Austrian Empire. It was within this period when his mother was diagnosed with breast cancer, but even his mother's condition couldn't convince young Adolf to cancel his plans of attending the Viennese Academy of Fine Arts. So, he left for Vienna in the early days of September 2017 and just a month later he was taking his admission tests for the art school. There were 113 candidates in total, but just twenty-eight of them were admitted into the Viennese Academy of Fine Arts. Adolf Hitler was not accepted at this prestigious academy, but he demanded an answer from the rector of this academy. He was told that his talent was not suitable for the school of painting. However, it could be helpful for architecture.

Adolf Hitler didn't want to let anyone from his hometown know about his failure, but a devastating blow determined him to return home. His mother's condition was deteriorating very fast, although the family doctor was paying special attention to her. On December 21, 1907, Klara Hitler died, leaving behind a griefed family. Adolf was probably the most affected by his mother's passing away because he lost the person who was closest to him and to whom he felt the most affection. This unfortunate event awakened the ambition in young Hitler, as now he had to face the harsh reality. He went back to Vienna for the third time with the ambition of becoming an architect.

The First Extremists Beliefs

In February 1908, after less than two months after his mother passed away, young Adolf left for Vienna for the third time. His new ambition was to become an architect, as he was now aware of his social condition. The money saved after his father died, was mostly spent on the treatment of his mother and now Adolf had little savings, and he had to work for a living. However, he never let go of his dreams of becoming a great artist, so he still lived in the same way he previously did in Vienna. Adolf Hitler lived in Vienna for the next five years, but those years marked the changing of an era. The great European city was the scene of political, cultural, social, and ethnic tensions, each of them leaving their mark on an impressionable young man coming from the provincial town of Linz to the great Austrian capital. It is within this period that the experiences he has in Vienna will shape the extremist beliefs that he will later show in his evolution.

Young Adolf benefited from a small orphan pension, which could barely cover his living expenses in Vienna. Although he was facing hunger and poverty, he did absolutely nothing to change his situation, as being bound to a job was not something that he could bear. Most of his time was spent in operas, Schönbrunn Palace, or within the center of the city (Ringstrasse). Being an architecture fanatic, he still spent a lot of time just gazing at the buildings in Vienna. His other main interest was opera, with Richard Wagner as his favorite composer. Of all Wagner's works, he found Lohengrin the best one, as he attended ten performances of this musical drama. A friend of Hitler from Linz (August Kubizek) joined him in Vienna to pursue the same Viennese Academic of Fine Arts. Unlike Hitler, he managed to get into this Academy to study music. Adolf Hitler preferred to paint for a living, and this is how he met Reinhold Hanisch, the person who helped him sell his paintings.

At the beginning of the twentieth century, Vienna was a multi-ethnic metropolis, but also the stage of ethnic, social, and political tensions. Adolf Hitler was exposed to all these tensions and was getting familiarized with the racist rhetoric. During this period he developed an admiration for Karl Lueger and Georg Ritter von Schönerer, two German nationalists with anti-Semitic ideas. His friend from Linz, August Kubizek was convinced that Hitler was an anti-Semite before leaving Linz for Vienna, but Reinhold Hanisch thought that only in Vienna young Adolf developed his anti-Semitic beliefs. He felt he had to move to a more Germanic city, as he felt only hate and contempt towards the Jews of Vienna.

In 1913 he decided to make this change and after receiving the last share of his father's estate, he moved to Munich in Germany. He was invited to join the Austro-Hungarian Army and was called for medical exams. On February 5, 1914, Hitler traveled to Salzburg for these exams, but he was considered unfit for military service. However, he wasn't disappointed as he didn't want to serve in this army with other nationalities, as he later concluded that the mixture of race and ethnic groups was the cause of the collapse of the Austro-Hungarian Empire. Adolf Hitler returned to Munich, where he lived until the beginning of World War I.

During that time, Munich was a vibrant city in which young Hitler felt he belonged. Although he was very impressed by the architecture of Vienna, he felt that the German population of the Austrian Empire was in danger due to the pro-Slav policies conducted by the authorities. Also, Hitler considered Vienna a "Babylon of races" and the mixture of all these foreign people was leading to the destruction of German culture. In Munich, he truly felt at home and the fifteen months he spent there just before the beginning of World War I was probably the happiest of his life. He felt that everything he knew from Wagner's operas, everything he fantasized about the German culture was real and right in front of his eyes. With impressive architecture and vibrant social life, Munich seemed to be Hitler's kind of city. A place in which he could continue living without having to work, or in which he could check the pulse of the city by going to the beer halls, opera, or theatre. It was the city that he could call home, the right place for a fanatic German nationalist (although he had spent his life in Austria so far).

Chapter 2
World War I Decorated Soldier

"I opened the document with trembling hands; no words of mine can describe the satisfaction I felt...Within a few days, I was wearing that uniform which I was not to put off again for nearly 6 years."

– Adolf Hitler, Mein Kampf p.147 (after receiving the reply after sending the petition to King Ludwig the III of Bavaria to join the Bavarian regiment as a volunteer, although he had Austrian citizenship)

a) Volunteer in the German Army

The beginning of the war symbolized the perfect opportunity for Adolf Hitler to prove himself as a nationalist. He felt that the war was for Germany's survival and future. He didn't hesitate to enroll as a volunteer in the Bavarian Army. Even Bavarian authorities acknowledged that Hitler's enrollment was most likely an administrative error. Since he was an Austrian citizen, he should have returned to Austria. He was allowed to serve in the Bavarian Reserve Infantry Regiment 16 as a dispatch runner, being responsible for delivering the messages to officers on the front line. He was stationed at Fournes-en-Weppes, the headquarters of this regiment which operated on the Western Front in Belgium and France. Adolf Hitler was not in the trenches fighting the enemy, but he spent a large portion of the war on the front or not far behind it.

His official title in the Bavarian Army was Meldegänger, the soldier responsible for carrying messages between the Regiment's Headquarters and the Company. Just after the First Battle of Ypres, from October-November 1914, Adolf Hitler was promoted to the position of corporal, or Gefreiter in German terms. Although he had ambitions to become a non-commissioned officer or Unteroffizier, this was his last promotion in World War I.

b) Battles and Decorations

Hitler was familiarized with the horrors of war during his military service on the Western Front. As a dispatch runner, he had plenty of time to pursue art activities, as he drew instructions and cartoons for the army newspapers. As usual, he wasn't the friendly kind, so he barely had any friends in his regiment. Instead, he was active enough on the front, where he delivered messages during the First Battle of Ypres, the Battle of the Somme, the Battle of Arras and the Battle of Passchendaele. During the Battle of the Somme, a shell exploded in the runners' dugout, causing the young Gefreiter an injury on his left thigh. After this unfortunate incident, he was sent for medical care at the Hospital in Beelitz, where he spent almost two months. On March 5, 1917, Adolf Hitler returned to his regiment and continued delivering messages as he did before. On October 15, 1918, he was attacked with mustard gas which led to temporary blindness. He was treated at Pasewalk hospital, where he found out about Germany's capitulation. When he heard of this news, he suffered from temporary blindness a second time.

His acts of bravery didn't go unnoticed as he received a few military decorations during the time he spent on the Western Front. In 1914, he was awarded the Iron Cross, second class and on August 4,

1918, he was awarded the Iron Cross first class, at the recommendation of his Jewish officer, Lieutenant Hugo Gutmann. Such decoration is rarely awarded to a Gefreiter, but Hitler convinced the superiors that he was worthy of the decoration. He also received the Black Wound Badge on May 18, 1918. Although he was a decorated soldier, Adolf Hitler was not promoted to a superior position. His superior officers thought that he lacked the necessary leadership skills. Also, being an introvert and of a different nationality was also a disadvantage for him to get promoted to Unteroffizier.

c) The Beginning of a New Ideology

Hitler considered World War I as the greatest of his experiences, but it was also the time during which his German nationalist feelings were nurtured. As he was recovering from the mustard gas attack in the Pasewalk hospital, he found out about Germany's surrender. He couldn't accept that an army which was never defeated in the front, would surrender itself to the enemy. The end of World War I marked the age of an era when empires collapsed under the pressure of new nationalities. The Austro-Hungarian Empire collapsed, as well as the Ottoman and the German Empire. In the East, the Russian Empire collapsed under the pressure of Bolshevism. All the inferior nations that Hitler despised had emerged from this conflict victorious. The map of Europe suffered significant changes, and the German state suffered a massive humiliation.

Hitler, just like other German patriots felt that Germany was betrayed by political leaders, Marxists, and Jews and all those who signed the armistice that stopped the fighting. They would be later referred to as the "November criminals." However, the real drama for Germany started after the treaty of Versailles, a humiliating and unjust peace treaty signed between Germany and the Allied Powers. This document imposed severe economic sanctions on Germany, as well as reparation costs to be paid. Also, Germany lost some territories and had to demilitarize the Rhineland region. Most of the German patriots would strongly disagree with Article 231 of the Treaty of Versailles, as it was interpreted as though Germany was responsible for the war.

The hate towards Jews and Marxists, which Hitler considered responsible for Germany's surrender nurtured his political ambitions and would mark his political path from then on. The Dolchstosslegende or the stab-in-the-back myth guided his future political career. He felt the German people were being wronged by these politicians and somebody needed to step up and raise Germany from its ashes.

Chapter 3
A Young and Ambitious Politician

"The force whichever set in motion the great historical avalanches of religious and political movements is the magic power of the spoken word. The broad masses of a population are more amenable to the appeal of rhetoric than to any other force."

– Adolf Hitler, Mein Kampf, p. 100

a) A New Voice for the Deutsche Arbeiterpartei

After the war, Hitler returned to Munich, to discover that the city he loved and felt most like home was changed. The transition after the war was very chaotic, especially on the political scene. Bavaria was ruled by the revolutionary Bavarian government, which acted as a National Council. This institution was controlled by radical parties like the Social Democrats or the Independent Social Democrats. The head of the government, Kurt Eisner, a radical Jew, was assassinated in the spring of 1919, leading to chaos on the Bavarian political scene. In April, Munich was overrun by communists who considered Moscow as a political model. The city had to be freed from the Soviet rule, and this mission was carried out by the Reichswehr troops (army) and Freikorps (volunteers). Hitler was no stranger to the contra-revolutionary activity, being involved in this process. Having reached almost thirty years of age with no skills or studies, therefore no potential career prospects, he decided to remain in the army. His experience on the front helped him obtain a position as an intelligence agent in Munich.

Therefore, he was given a new mission, to infiltrate within the ranks of a small political party called the German Workers' Party or Deutsche Arbeiterpartei (DAP). Acknowledging his oratorical skills, his superiors within the army hoped that he could become a populist agitator (while still being in the army service) within this tiny party, which they thought was radical. As much of the politics was discussed in beer halls, Hitler was present at political debates within these social places. He had proven his oratorical skills and at a DAP meeting on September 12, 1919, he got the full attention of the Party's Chairman, Anton Drexler. Hitler received a copy of *My Political Awakening*, which is a political manifest containing anti-capitalism, anti-Marxism, and especially, anti-Semitic ideas. Encouraged by his army superiors, Hitler joined the DAP and became the party member 555 (apparently the DAP started counting members at five hundred, to give the impression they were a much larger party).

Just a few days later, Hitler had written his first recorded statement related to the Jews in the Gemlich letter. He writes that the government goal should be the removal of all Jews. Suddenly, Hitler was starting to feel more important and appreciated, as his speeches reached more and more people. One of the most important party members of DAP was Dietrich Eckart, who was one of the party's founding members, but also a member of the Thule Society which is an occult organization. Eckart took Hitler under his wing and became his mentor. He also introduced Hitler to Munich's high society. With Eckart and Hitler working together, the DAP was slowly becoming more popular.

b) Birth of the Nazi Party

The year 1920 marked the birth of the Nazionalsozialistische Deutsche Arbeiterpartei NSDAP (National Socialist German Working Party). Hitler was responsible for drawing the party's logo, the swastika within a white circle and with a red background. At this point, he was beyond the political agitator; therefore he was discharged by the army and started to work full-time for the Nazi party. With the help of Dietrich Eckart, Hitler became an even better speaker, capable of manipulating huge crowds. The headquarters of the Nazi party were in Munich, which at that time was the "wasps nest" for anti-Marxists and anti-government German nationalists. Their main goal was to destroy Marxism and to end the Weimar Republic. By February 1921, Hitler was already a master speaker, giving a speech to the assistance of more than 6000. Prior to the meeting, a few party supporters were spread all over Munich handing out leaflets and waving the swastika. The crowd was simply mesmerized by Hitler's energy, but also by his critical speech towards rival politicians, Treaty of Versailles, but mostly against Marxists and Jews.

A bigger party didn't mean a united party; many fellow party colleagues didn't recognize Hitler as a leader. Some of the leading party members wanted to merge with the German Socialist Party, but at this point, Hitler resigned from the party. They realized that without Hitler, the Nazi party would lose its most prominent and public figure. The condition for a comeback was the replacement of Anton Drexler as party chairman. Those leaders agreed, and Hitler rejoined the Nazi Party as member 3680 on 26th July. There were still some opponents in the party, who spread a pamphlet which categorized Hitler as a traitor. However, at the party's congress on July 29, he was voted chairman with 533 in favor to one against, replacing Anton Drexler.

The party members were omnipresent in the beer halls of Munich, where there were countless speeches given by Hitler. His message in the speeches was simple, and it reached out to plenty of people. The energy, the gesture, the tone of his voice, all contributed to the hypnotic effect of the speech. He abused the popular themes, talking about the politicians responsible for the economic hardship, the Treaty of Versailles, and how Jews and Marxists caused Germany's suffering. In those times, this was the kind of speech which captivated the crowd.

Soon after the establishment of the Nazi party, their political program was released. It included twenty-five points, and even today it can't be considered an ideology of a party because it lacks the coherence for it. The Pan-Germanic movement inspired these ideas, and it included some aspects like opposition towards the Treaty of Versailles, some socialist ideas, anti-capitalism, anti-Semitism and ultranationalism. The program was also considered a tool of propaganda, and it proved to be very useful in attracting new members.

Some of the most important Nazi members were Rudolf Hess, Hermann Göring, and Ernst Röhm. The last one was handed the task of creating the SA (Stormtroopers) as the Nazi Party feared paramilitary organization, responsible for protecting meetings and attacking opponent politicians. By this time, the party was growing in size, attracting not only members but also new sponsors. Hitler's hatred towards the Jews was also amplified by the influence the Aufbau Vereinigung had on him. This was a conspirational group of Russians who were opposed to the Bolsheviks, who were convinced that there was a Jewish conspiracy behind the rise of Bolshevism, as the Jewish international finance was connected with this movement.

The Beer Hall Putsch

If 1919 was a year of local political chaos in Munich, being ended by the Reichswehr intervention alongside the Freikorps, a few years later tensions grew as people did not accept the draconic measures imposed by the Treaty of Versailles. The Republic of Weimar was too weak to control these tensions and in times like those radical ideas were in people's minds. In Munich, the Nazi Party felt like the communists were trying to seize power, so Hitler thought this was the time to act. Although the whole nation was unified by the French occupation of the Ruhr area from the beginning of 1923, the authorities in Berlin thought that passive resistance would be enough in this situation.

In this year the Nazi party intensified its activity, with Hitler giving more speeches in beer halls. The goal of the party right now was to gain control of Munich and to march on Berlin in an attempt to seize power. Hitler was inspired by Benito Mussolini's "March on Rome", a coup initiated in Italy by "Il Duce" which was successful as he was named the prime minister. Hitler felt this was the time to react, although his party was unknown outside Bavaria. He was planning on taking control over Munich and Bavaria and then march on Berlin to challenge the government. However, to get the control over Munich, he would need the support of three key figures in Munich: the State Commissioner Gustav Ritter von Kahr, the Chief of Police Hans Ritter von Seisser and the Reichswehr General Otto von Lossow. Kahr already had almost dictatorial powers over Bavaria and lately had banned most of the public meetings of any party, fearing of a putsch from the Left wing or Right wing extremists.

Returned from his exile in Sweden, Erich von Ludendorff was a former army general, a living legend amongst Germans, who never lost a battle in World War I, but was sabotaged by the politicians on the "home front." Hitler knew that to achieve his plans, Ludendorff was the person to get on his side, as he was still a well-respected person amongst the army's officers and also amongst the politicians of the Bavarian Government. During this year, Hitler managed to get Ludendorff by his side and at this point, he was trying to get support from the three persons who held all the power in Bavaria. Seeking for the right opportunity, the Nazis found out that there was a public meeting on November 8, 1923, in the Bürgerbräukeller beer hall where all these three key figures were attending. Hitler, a few Nazi members, and the SA stormed into the beer hall and interrupted Kahr's speech in front of 3000 people, announcing the beginning of a national revolution and declaring the formation of a new government with General Erich von Ludendorff as a key figure. Hitler demanded support from Kahr, Seisser, and Lossow and he received it. The Nazi members managed to occupy the local headquarters of the Reichswehr and the Police. The next day, Hitler and his Nazi followers planned to march from the beer hall to the Bavarian War Ministry, in his attempt to overthrow the Bavarian government, but Kahr, Seisser, and Lossow withdrew their support, so neither the army nor the police joined Hitler's forces. Instead, the Nazi members and the SA were dispersed by the police in this attempt to seize power in Bavaria. Sixteen of the Nazi members were killed in this attempt, while four police officers died in the gunfire.

Hitler managed to escape and flew to Ernst Hanfstaengl house where he was hiding. Just a few days later, on November 11, 1923, he was arrested for high treason. In February 1924, his trial began at the People's Court and on April 1 1924, Hitler received his sentence of five years at Landsberg Prison. The Nazi Party was left in the hands of

Alfred Rosenberg, who acted as the temporary leader. It was in prison that he wrote Mein Kampf, a book comprising all the anti-Semitic and anti-Marxist ideas he had. The book presents Jews as parasites and as "international poisoners" of society. According to it, the only solution was the complete extermination of the Jews, but the book didn't make any reference about this process and what it consists of. Between 1925 and 1932, Mein Kampf was sold in more than 228 thousand copies and in 1932 and 1933, the book was sold in one million copies. He wasn't mistreated in Landsberg Prison as he received special and friendly treatment from the guards, as well as visits and letters from fellow Nazi members, especially his deputy, Rudolf Hess.

On December 20, 1924, Hitler was released from Landsberg prison after spending less than nine months imprisoned there. The Bavarian Supreme Court pardoned him, and despite the state prosecutor's objections, Hitler was again free and determined more than ever to seize power and control over Germany. However, this time he would plan more meticulously before attempting to seize power because the Beer Hall Putsch was more of an instinct reaction, a now or never situation in which he thought it was the right time to act. This coup wasn't the result of a very meticulous plan, and Hitler had time to contemplate in prison about what went wrong. Instead of rushing to power, as the Nazis did before the failed coup, Hitler would dedicate his time to organize and build the Nazi party in order to become the strongest political force in all of Germany.

The Bavarian government tried to deport Hitler back to Austria, because now were they aware of the administrative error that was made when they allowed Hitler to join the Bavarian Reserve Regiment in World War I. However, the request was denied by the Austrian federal chancellor, claiming that the military service in the German Army made Hitler's Austrian citizenship void. On April 7, 1925, Hitler officially renounced his Austrian citizenship, as now he was busy rebuilding the Nazi party.

A Short message from the Author:

Hey, are you enjoying the book? I'd love to hear your thoughts!

Many readers do not know how hard reviews are to come by, and how much they help an author.

I would be incredibly grateful if you could take just 60 seconds to write a brief review on Amazon, even if it's just a few sentences!

>> Click here to leave a quick review

https://www.amazon.com/review/create-review?asin=XXXXXXXXX

Thank you for taking the time to share your thoughts!

Your review will genuinely make a difference for me and help gain exposure for my work.

Chapter 4
Pursuit of Power

"I cast my eyes back to the time when with six other unknown men I founded this association, when I spoke before eleven, twelve, thirteen, fourteen, twenty, thirty, fifty persons. When I recall how after a year I had won sixty-four members for the movement, I must confess that that which has today been created, when a stream of millions is flowing into our movement, represents something unique in German history. The bourgeois parties have had seventy years to work in. Where is the organization which in seventy years has achieved what we have achieved in barely twelve?"

– Adolf Hitler's speech at the Industry Club in Düsseldorf, January 27, 1932

a) The Years After the Prison Release

The consequences of the Beer Hall Putsch were catastrophic for the Nazi Party, as the party was banned all over Bavaria. By the time of Hitler's release, the political scene was less combative, and the economy had improved, meaning there were fewer opportunities for Hitler's political agitations. Not only was the party banned, but their voice in the press, the newspaper Völkischer Beobacher was also prohibited. Some of the Nazi party leaders fled abroad (Hermann Göring only returned in 1927), while others were killed by the gunshots during the putsch, or died soon after. Hitler's mentor, Dietrich Eckart died at the end of 1923, so the party was left without leaders in this period. Hitler had chosen Alfred Rosenberg to handle the party affairs, but now the party was banned because of the failed putsch. He wasn't a leader, so Hitler felt that his position within the party was not threatened by Rosenberg, as he was no man of action and couldn't impose any authority.

During Hitler's imprisonment, there was a conflict between Rosenberg and the more radical side of the party represented by Julius Streicher and Hermann Esser. Adolf Hitler didn't want the party to flourish without him, so he didn't choose any side of this conflict. Leaders like Rosenberg, Ludendorff, Strasser, or Röhm were determined to participate in the state and national elections of spring 1924. At this point Hitler was consumed by radical ideas which lead to the writing of Mein Kampf, so he was against any democratic or parliamentary activity. He was worried about his position within the party if other leaders of the party would be elected in the Reichstag. As the party was outside of the law, Nazi leaders could get a candidate only through Völkisch groups. (people's groups). Leaders like Rosenberg, Ludendorff, Strasser, Feder, Röhm, and Frick ran on the list of the National Socialist German Freedom Movement, which was just a minor people's group amongst the Völkisch bloc, which became the second largest political power in the Reichstag. The Nazis managed to secure thirty-two positions in the German Parliament (Reichstag), being just a minor success of the elections of April and May 1924. Hitler was still too skeptical about this success, but for Ludendorff and Strasser, it was an encouragement to strengthen the alliance the Nazis of Bavaria had with the North German Deutsch-völkische Freitheitspartei, a radical party from Northern Germany, led by Albrecht von Graefe and Graf Ernst zu Reventlow, who shared the same radical views as the Bavarian Nazis (ultranationalist, racist and anti-Semitic ideas). Hitler was against any alliance, as he felt that such arrangements might alter the purpose and vigor of the party. Also, he was too concerned with his position in the party, as these Nazi leaders did not consider his opinion. He preferred a small party, but pure, which he could easily control. In Mein Kampf, Hitler was convinced that the strong is strongest when it's alone.

Another cause of frustration for Hitler was the earlier release of Ernst Röhm, who quickly started building the Frontbann, the stormtroopers at a different scale. The organization grew very fast, having thousands of recruits, from different regions, including East Prussia and Austria. The SA was originally conceived to intimidate political opponents and for propaganda, and although it was well organized it started to become very difficult to control. Hitler feared that the actions of Röhm would delay his release from jail.

As the economy was starting to work again and there were elections again for the Reichstag, the votes for the Nazi people bloc fell dramatically, and only 14 Nazi politicians obtained a seat in the Parliament. Hitler avoided deportation to Austria while he was in prison, so now he could focus on rebuilding the party. Some of the leaders like Rosenberg, Ludendorff, and Röhm fell into disgrace, and Hitler was very determined to rebuild the party and increase the propaganda activity. Just two months after his release, the Völksicher Beobachter appeared again, having a consistent editorial signed by Hitler. But the Nazis were not quite prepared to let him lead the party. It was only after his speech on February 27, 1925, at the Bürgerbräukeller beer hall, that all the remaining Nazi enthusiasts recognized him as the rightful leader. This marked the re-birth of the Nazi Party and with it Hitler had two main goals, to remove any existent opponent within the party and to build a political force within the legal framework. Like the Phoenix, the Nazi party had risen from its own ashes. In the same place which marked its defeat and ban, the party had been re-founded.

The Presidential elections of 1925 marked a total failure for the Nazi party, as their candidate, Erich von Ludendorff only obtained 211 thousand votes out of twenty-seven million. At this point, Hitler realized that Ludendorff was no longer an asset for him, so the former World War I general fell into disgrace. At this point, the Nazis supported Field-Marshal von Hindenburg, a last-minute candidate brought by the nationalists who won by a very small margin. The economy was still recovering, so Hitler's topics were not very popular outside the German Nationalists. Since he was against any political alliances, Hitler trusted Joseph Goebbels, and also the Strasser brothers (Gregor and Otto) to develop and enlarge the party in the northern part of Germany. However, the odds were against the political ambitions of Hitler, as funding for the party was very difficult to find and at the parliamentary elections of 1928, the party only received 2.6 percent of the votes, a total of 810100 votes. Hitler's speeches didn't reach out to the mass crowds, as people were no longer finding themselves in this rhetoric. However, the Nazis tried to become more present in social life, organizing festivities, but without gaining too much popularity.

However, Hitler's luck was about to change with the collapse of the global economy. The Crash of 1929 was the perfect opportunity for Hitler and his henchmen to rise to power. Germany was severely affected by this crisis, as unemployment went to the rough, more than six million Germans being now in this condition. Banks collapsed and people's money and savings were in danger. Hitler had the answer for who was responsible for this and repeated this in all of his speeches. However, they also promised solutions for the crisis, like strengthening the economy, providing jobs for the unemployed, and also breaking the Treaty of Versailles. With such popular themes and powerful speeches, the Nazis were able to climb to power, as the elections of September 1930 allowed this party to become a major political power in the Reichstag.

The Nazi Party Becomes a Power in the Reichstag

The Great Depression was the perfect opportunity for extremists to become popular and in some cases to come to power. It was also the time when the Nazis gained the most supporters. The Strasser brothers were very successful in developing the party in the northern part of Germany, but also Hitler made some new connections, like Otto Dietrich, who owned a nationwide press agency. Hitler's speeches were now available across the nation and he was becoming known in all of Germany. Until now, he was only known in Bavaria, but Germans from other parts knew little to nothing about him. Otto Dietrich was the son-in-law of the political advisers of the Mining Union in the Ruhr area and the owner of Rheinisch-Westfälische Zeitung, the newspaper of the Ruhr area industrialists. This was how Hitler met Emil Kirdorf, one of the most important names of the German industry. He was the person controlling all the funds for the Mining Union.

Hitler managed to secure funds for his party and his plan to overthrow the government had now a chance to succeed. His speeches and ideas could now reach a much wider audience, and he got the party involved in celebrations and even charity events. They provided food and entertainment for many Germans. All these actions were not in vain and the results were soon to come with the elections for the Reichstag in September 1930. The Nazi party received more than 6.4 million votes, meaning 18.3 percent of the total votes. These elections were a massive blow to the centered parties, as the Nazis secured 107 positions in the Reichstag (making them the second political force of Germany) and other extremist parties also received a considerable amount of seats in the German Parliament. Hindenburg, the elected president, didn't want to hand over the power to extremist parties. Therefore a minority cabinet was installed, which had a puppet chancellor named Heinrich Brüning from the Centre Party. The Brüning administration was just a softer phase of dictatorship because the chancellor was governing through emergency decrees direct from the president. Therefore, this administration had to impose austerity measures, while Germans continued to lose their jobs, and most of the inflation was affecting everyone living in Germany.

It took almost seven years since Hitler renounced his Austrian citizenship until he received the German citizenship granted by Dietrich Klagges, who was a member of the Nazi party, but also the interior minister of Brunswick. On February 25th, 1932, Hitler was officially made a citizen of Brunswick, thus becoming a German citizen. It was perfect timing, as Hitler was now running for the presidency against the independent candidate, Paul von Hindenburg, the current president of Germany. Even though Hitler was the runner-up on both rounds, (on March 13, and April 10, 1932) his defeat was compensated by the tremendous success of the Nazi party in the Reichstag elections from July 1932. The party secured 37.3 percent of the total votes, with not less than 13.74 million votes. Therefore, the Nazi party had now 230 seats in the German Parliament. The center parties were on a downfall, as the austerity measures had severe consequences over a large amount of the German population. Paul von Hindenburg's main candidates in his electoral campaign were Hitler and Ernst Thälmann (the leader of the KPD, the German Communist Party). In the Reichstag elections, most of the seats were secured by extremist parties even though Hindenburg called for another vote for parliamentary elections in November 1932, just a few months after the Nazi's tremendous success in the previous elections. Hindenburg's hopes for a majority government soon faded after the results of the Reichstag elections. Even though it lost a few places in the Parliament, the Nazi party remained the main political force, with 196 seats.

Hitler was supported by German industrialists, who saw in him the only capable person of restoring Germany to its former glory. Some of the most influential politicians like Franz von Papen and Alfred Hugenberg were also supporting Hitler, and they wrote a letter to Hindenburg trying to persuade him to name Hitler the chancellor of Germany. Hindenburg considered this proposition and on January 30, 1933, named Hitler as the new chancellor, but the cabinet was formed by only three   Nazi members: Adolf Hitler (chancellor), Wilhelm Frick (Minister of the Interior) and Hermann Göring, who was appointed the Minister of the Interior for Prussia. Hitler received what he wanted, the chancellor position and the control of police all over Germany.

Fall of the Weimar Republic

The Weimar Republic, a form of government designated to restore the order and guide Germany through the difficult years to come, was the result of the Kaiser's abdication in November 1918. The politicians had to implement the decisions of the Treaty of Versailles, including the loss of territories, harsh economic sanctions, and demilitarization of the Rhine region. It wasn't an easy job, as they had to deal with hyperinflation, massive unemployment, and social turmoil. This republic had two presidents, who were in service for a longer period. The first one was Friedrich Ebert, who acted as president from February 11, 1919, to February 28. 1925. The other one was Paul von Hindenburg, who served as president from May 12, 1925, to August 2, 1934.

Although this form of organization had numerous advantages like democracy, the power being held by the government and the bill of rights, it also had two major disadvantages. The first one was proportional representation, meaning that each party could get a number of seats in the Reichstag according to the percentage of votes received. This meant that every party who gathered some votes (it did not matter how many) could get seats in the parliament and therefore block laws. Also, governments were very vulnerable to this form of organization, as they would fall on many occasions if there wasn't a majority in the Reichstag to support them. The second issue with the Weimar Republic is Article 48, which gave the president dictatorial powers in case of emergency and could act without the Reichstag approval. President Paul von Hindenburg used this right in the Brüning administration.

The extremist parties were a very serious threat to the republic, as there were some attempts to overthrow the government in a non-democratic way. However, as the economic situation of Germany got very bad and unemployment was very high, the left and right wing parties (the extremists) gained a lot of votes and supporters. They easily started to fill the seats of the Reichstag, making it very difficult to pass laws, especially the ones issued by the Centre parties. The Great Depression was the devastating blow to the Weimar Republic because it gave reasons for political agitators to thrive and gain support from large crowds. As the central authorities were too gentle to handle the extremists, the communist and the ultranationalist movement were developing at a very large scale.

As the German politicians were collaborating with politicians of the Allies to reach an agreement related to the war debts Germany still had to pay the Allies, most of the German nationalists were outraged about the amount of money the country had to pay as compensation to the Allies. Radical politicians even initiated a referendum, which had the purpose of breaking the Treaty of Versailles and make a criminal offense of the cooperation of German politicians for collecting any reparations. Although this referendum was initiated on December 22, 1929, as a consequence of the Young Plan, Germans were not very interested in voting at this referendum, because less than 15 percent of the people voted. This failed attempt only fuelled Hitler's ambitions to seize power to amend the injustice that was done to Germany.

Running in the elections for President, made Hitler realize the German people's reaction towards him and his ideas. His campaign entitled "Hitler über Deutschland" (Hitler over Germany) was a success, although he lost the elections in favor of Paul von Hindenburg. Without any doubts, he was amongst the first politicians to use the airplane for political purposes, being able to travel to the most important cities of Germany and hypnotize the audience with his energic speeches. He received almost 37 percent of the total votes, but the Nazi party became the biggest name on the political scene of Germany.

The Reichstag elections of July and November 1932 proved to Hindenburg that the Nazis were the strongest political force of Germany, and there wasn't enough support in the Reichstag for a central government. Persuaded by Franz von Papen and Alfred Hugenberg, two of the most influential politicians of that period, Hindenburg named Adolf Hitler as chancellor of Germany. Hitler also managed to secure two other seats in his cabinet for fellow party members. Therefore Wilhelm Frick was named the Minister of Interior, while Hermann Göring was appointed Minister of Interior for Prussia. Thus, the Nazi party took control of the police in Germany.

Hitler planned his seizure of power very meticulously, like a skilled chess player, and after becoming chancellor, he eliminated his political opponents. Step by step, he gained more power and slowly took most of the power Hindenburg had. The year 1933 marked the beginning of Hitler's dictatorship, but it was only in 1934 when he proclaimed himself Führer after the death of Hindenburg when the Weimar Republic had officially ended.

Although it was intended as a democratic form of organization, the final days of the Weimar Republic were closer to dictatorship than democracy. All the power was concentrated in the hands of Hindenburg, Papen and Schleicher and they had support from the biggest industrialists, estate-owners and the army. All these lobby groups mostly have different interests; however, all of them were interested in overthrowing the constitutional party system, the crush of Marxism and trade unions, but also they were interested in restoring a form of authoritarianism. This was the common ground for these elite groups, which were supporting different parties. Since the democratic elections for the Reichstag didn't offer any conclusive result, because there was no party having a majority, they had to select one of the great political leaders to guide Germany to an authoritarian regime. The leader they were looking for turned up to be Adolf Hitler, who now had the masses with him and just was a figure not to be ignored.

It can be said that the Weimar Republic collapsed because of the hard consequences of the Great Depression which were affecting Germany, but the tombstone of this political regime was placed by the lobby groups, which handpicked the perfect person to destroy this form of organization and lead this country to a more autocratic regime. By the time Hitler was named chancellor, the Weimar Republic was in a coma and it died at the same time with its President.

Chapter 5
Chancellor of a Weakened Germany

"The struggle is a light one now since we are able to employ all the means of the State. Radio and Press are at our disposal. We shall achieve a masterpiece of propaganda. Even money is not lacking this time."

— Joseph Goebbels

Rise to Power

Now that Hitler was in power, he did everything he could to consolidate it, by working against his political opponents in order to achieve the majority in the Reichstag to support his government. Hitler would need other parliamentary elections to achieve this goal. However, something extraordinary needed to happen to call for other elections. On February 27, 1933, the Reichstag building was burnt, an incident for which the Nazis blamed the communists. Hitler convinced Hindenburg to act under Article 48 and to issue the Reichstag Fire Decree, a law which suspended any rights and permitted detention without any trial. This gave the perfect opportunity for the SA (having more than two million members) to go after the communist party members and engage in anti-communist violence. All the activities of the German Communist Party (KPD) were prohibited and more than four thousand KPD members were arrested.

Parliamentary elections were announced for March 6, 1933, which gave the Nazi party a good reason to intensify the anti-communist propaganda in the previous days before the elections. The propaganda paid off, as the Nazis had 43.9 percent of the total votes resulting in 288 seats in the Reichstag. However, it still wasn't enough to have a majority government, so the Nazis were obliged to form a coalition with the DNVP. March 21, 1933, was the beginning of the new Reichstag, which was celebrated with an opening ceremony at Potsdam. Since he achieved the majority only by having an alliance with a different party, Hitler wasn't planning to use the alliance, as he didn't trust any alliance with another party. Instead, his cabinet issued the Enabling Act or Gesetz zur Behebung der Not von Volk und Reich (or The Law to Remedy the Distress of People and Reich), which gave Hitler the right to issue laws for four years without the approval of the Reichstag. This law passed the Reichstag with 441 in favor and 84 against, and under these circumstances Hitler became the dictator of Germany.

He had full power and to consolidate it, he started suppressing his political opponents. The "Iron Fist" of the Nazi party, the stormtroopers were responsible for intimidating all the politicians who opposed the Nazi party. Hitler was aware that he had to take control over the working class. Therefore he dissolved all the trade unions and arrested all their leaders. The Nazis created the German Labour Front, an organization which was meant to represent the company owners, administrators, and workers.

Hitler also directed his SA troops to intimidate the Nazis coalition partner, the DNVP, convincing its leader (Alfred Hugenberg), to resign on June 29, 1933. Taking care of all other political opponents, and also allies, Hitler declared that the Nazi party was the only legal, political entity in Germany (July 14, 1933). In the ranks of his own party, as there were still some members who were opposing him, he conducted a purge within the Nazi party. However, this process had to be directed to the SA as well, because he felt that it had become an organization very difficult to control, undisciplined, and which consumed large resources. The stormtroopers were a threat to political, military, and industrial leaders and Hitler felt that this organization had been diverted from his true purpose. Actions were necessary, so Hitler arranged for the assassination of Ernst Röhm and other SA leaders, and also for other politicians like Gregor Strasser and Kurt von Schleicher. This purge was called the Night of the Long Knives, and it took place from between June 30, 1934, to July 2, 1934.

▌Führer

On August 2, 1934, the death of President Hindenburg also marked the death of the Weimar Republic. However, just one day before, Hitler issued the "Law concerning the Highest State Office of the Reich," which stipulated the abolishment of the office of president and merging its powers with those of the chancellor. This law made Hitler the Head of State, and also the Head of the Government. He was formally named Führer and Reichskanzler, but the last title he quickly renounced. At this point, nobody in Germany could overthrow Hitler, as now he was the supreme leader of this country.

The introverted Austrian who had no career perspectives over twenty-five years ago, had proclaimed himself as the Führer of Germany, a position which had all the power in Germany in one hand, whether it was executive, legislation, or military. He achieved all this power step by step, first by winning the votes of the people, then taking over the Reichstag, eliminating all his opponents within and outside the Nazi party and taking advantage of a president who was easy to manipulate. In August 1934, Hitler was perfectly positioned to follow his dream further and to correct the wrong which was done to Germany by the Treaty of Versailles and the Young Plan. It was his mission to guide Germany out of the Great Depression and direct it to a brighter and glorious future. It wasn't an easy task, but most of the Germans believed that he was the right man to take Germany on the right path.

From the early days of a political agitator, until he had become the supreme leader of Germany, he had evolved a lot. In the beginning, his audience was a small crowd in a beer hall, but now he had become a master capable of a live performance in front of hundreds of thousands. He was able to hypnotize the crowd with his beliefs and lure them to the Nazi side. His message was simple and it reached millions of Germans who found themselves in his words. The humble origins of Hitler (a commoner), was also something that helped him reach the crowds. As the German people lost the confidence in the ruling elite, which was considered to blame for the catastrophic effects of the Treaty of Versailles, they were hoping for a savior to lead Germany to glory again. The German people thought that this person could only come from amongst themselves because only such a person could experience exactly what they were experiencing.

Although his entrance into politics was somehow pushed by the army, as his mission was to infiltrate a radical party, he soon enjoyed this mission so much that he became a full-time politician. Giving speeches about the harsh times Germany was in, but also about the traitors who brought this country to its knees, he felt like he had found his true purpose, fighting to save Germany from Marxists and Jews. Only after spending 9 months in prison he became a more mature politician, as before the Beer Hall Putsch he had the impatience of a fanatic and young politician who wanted to rush himself to power. The failed coup would represent a devastating blow for the Nazi party, as it was banned for a period and although the party was re-founded in 1925, only starting with the Great Depression did the party increased in popularity.

After his release from prison, Hitler started consolidating his power within the party and also laid the foundation of a bigger, more organized party spread all across Germany. He started using propaganda at a different level, and his message reached out to millions of Germans. Hitler also involved the party in community activities, making the people aware of the party. He perfected his speech, and by the time Germany was having serious economic issues, people found his message as making the most sense. Gaining support from more people, powerful industrialists, and press agency owners is what transformed Hitler from a provincial politician to an important political figure known nationwide. The Great Depression helped the Nazi party rise to power, as by the time Hitler was running for President in 1932, his party was the strongest political organization throughout Germany. It took over the Reichstag in a democratic way and once in power, it eliminated all the other parties. Hitler was named chancellor, and he consolidated this position until he was the de facto dictator of Germany. The death of President Hindenburg meant that the final legal element which could take his power no longer existed, as he seized all the power in Germany to himself.

Consolidating Power

Now that he had all the power in Germany, Hitler started to implement his plan for the German people and to deliver what he promised. It was a time when the country was still suffering from unemployment, so he had to find a way to provide jobs for the poor and unemployed. A solution was the building of a massive network of motorways, or as the Germans would know it, "Autobahn," which provided work for many people. Hitler himself was trying to set an example, as video footages were showing him working side by side with the German people to build the autobahns. Motorways from today's Germany date back from Hitler's time. However, the Nazis didn't settle just for the motorways' they also built dams, a large network of railways and other civil works. As Hitler was preparing for the war, he encouraged the production of weapons for the army in the existent steel factories. All these measures meant more jobs for the German people, and even though the wages were lower compared to the ones from the Weimar Republic and an average German was working forty-seven to fifty hours per week, Hitler managed to control the working class and prevent any revolts.

The Nazi propaganda controlled the media and every message broadcast through the radio and also every article published in newspapers had to get the Nazi's approval. This is how the regime advertised only its achievements and hid from the public eye what was happening with the Jews or other social categories which the Nazis hated. The swastika was displayed everywhere and the official salute became "Heil Hitler," which also involved the gesture of raising the right hand into the air with a straightened hand.

Hitler wanted to create a regime powerful enough to last 1000 years. He always thought that the legacy of such a regime would be its architecture. As he was always passionate about architecture, he found a young architect who shared his visions and was capable of implementing Hitler's interpretation of the Classic German Culture. Albert Speer was the architect whom Hitler thought would be worthy of carrying out his plans. Therefore he was charged with the building renovations of Berlin. There was a massive architectural project with imposing buildings as a legacy of the Nazi regime, to completely transform Berlin as the greatest capital in the world.

The Olympic Games of 1936 hosted by Nazi Germany were the biggest opportunity to show to the world the progress of the country. Athletes from all over the world came to Berlin and competed in numerous sports competitions and many of them were performing the Nazi salute at the opening ceremony. Hitler had projected into the eyes of foreigners the image of a strong Germany which had recovered from the horrors of the past and now looked to a brighter future. It was also a clear message to its outside enemies and an attempt to strike fear into their heart, at the glimpse of the Nazi might. Unfortunately, this message was not received by Great Britain and France, which were not aware of Hitler's real intentions regarding foreign policy.

Hitler was intending to indoctrinate young Germans with the Nazi ideology. Therefore he paid extra attention to the younger generation, as he was convinced that through them the regime would last longer, perhaps for one thousand years. Therefore, he created Hitler's Youth, an organization which had the purpose of imposing the Nazi way of thinking to young boys. From the age of six, the young boys were sent to camps where they were formed in the Nazi way.

They had to go through rigorous physical training, as they were prepared first for the SA and eventually for the Wehrmacht (the German Army). By 1939, 90 percent of the German boys were already in Hitler's youth.

Girls were not forgotten by the Nazi regime, as the party had prepared something really special for them. Hitler created the League of German Girls, which actually was the feminine wing of Hitler's Youth. This organization was split into different groups like the Young Girls League (for girls between ten to fourteen years old) and another league for girls aged between fourteen and eighteen years old. In 1938, another section was added to the organization, called the Faith and Beauty League, which was open for girls between seventeen and twenty-one years old. This last section was basically preparing these young women for career goals, domestic life, and marriage, as they were encouraged to get married young and have children, but to have an education first and a career if possible. By doing this, Hitler wanted to lay the groundwork and sow the seeds of the Nazi movement and ideology for the future generations.

Chapter 6
Building the Military Power

"There is no solidarity in Europe; there is only submission"

– Adolf Hitler to Otto Strasser in 1927

▮Breaking the Treaty of Versailles

According to Hitler, the Treaty of Versailles was one of the biggest humiliations in German history, because not only did it mean the capitulation of Germany (which was not defeated in the front), but it also introduced very harsh sanctions on Germany. There were some significant territory losses for Germany, such as the loss of Alsace and Lorraine to France, a massive territory of East Prussia and Upper Silesia were lost in the favor of Poland, the city of Danzig was declared a free city, Saarland was placed under the supervision of the League of Nations and all the German colonies from the Pacific, China, and Africa were lost to Great Britain, France, and Japan.

As the Allies were making Germany responsible for the war, they also imposed huge reparation costs to be made for the damage the German Army had done during World War I. In 1921, the total reparation costs were set to thirty-three billion dollars, a sum which was incredibly high for that time. The treaty also gave the Allies power to act if the Germans fell back with payments, as the French and Belgians did in the region of Ruhr between January 11, 1923, and August 25, 1925. The French wanted to prevent any possible German retribution and to make sure that Germany would never be a military threat for Europe, by restricting the German Army to just one hundred thousand soldiers and eliminating the generals. The production of tanks, planes, submarines, cars, and poisonous gas was completely forbidden' just a small number of factories being allowed to manufacture weapons and ammunition. Also, the entire Rhineland had to be demilitarized. This treaty also meant the founding of the League of Nations, which was an organization very similar to today's UN, in which the members would guarantee the independence and territorial integrity of the other members. The sole purpose of the League of Nations was to preserve the peace.

Any German nationalist would be deeply offended by the radical sanctions imposed on Germany by the Allies, and this treaty caused massive social revolts. Such a treaty was, in fact, the birth certificate of radical nationalist movements in Germany and was responsible for the rise to power of the Nazi party. As the German people were suffering from unemployment and severe austerity measures imposed by the Weimar Republic, they were searching and expecting a political figure to break the Treaty of Versailles and to set right the wrong which was done to Germany. Hitler and all the German nationalists couldn't accept Germany's surrender, especially because its army was never defeated in the field, and they felt like the German Army was betrayed by cowardly politicians, the people Hitler liked to call the "criminals of November". If Germany's surrender was very hard for them to bear, the Treaty of Versailles was, in fact, the explosion which generated social revolts. Ever since his electoral campaign from 1932, Hitler promised to break the Treaty of Versailles and lead Germany back to its former glory.

In the Nazi ideology, the pure born German was considered a superior race compared to other nationalities, like the ones from the East (which Hitler hated so much, not just Jews, but also other Slavic nationalities, for which he had a growing hatred ever since the period he spent in Vienna). Führer's plan was to extend the Lebensraum, which means expanding the living space of the German people by conquering new territories and eliminate or turn into slaves the existing inferior population. Such a goal could only be obtained by war, which not only broke the Treaty of Versailles but also violated the rules of the League of Nations (of which Germany was a member).

Ever since the Nazis had risen to power, they had promised jobs for the unemployed Germans, and they managed to keep their promise as unemployment decreased from six million to just one million. The Nazi's revitalized the infrastructure, but also many of the jobs were in factories, which were now required to manufacture weapons, ammunition, tanks, airplanes, submarines, ships, and other war machines. Hitler brought back to life the weaponry industry by using the Mefo bills (a promissory note issued by the German Central Bank). Also, during this time the Nazi administration printed a lot of money and also seized the valuables of many Jews and also wealthy enemies of the State.

In 1933, Germany renounced its membership of the League of Nations and didn't participate at the World Disarmament Conference in October 1933. That should have been a very clear message to the world that Germany was preparing for war. However, the great powers didn't react, as they didn't react when 90 percent of the population in Saarland (which was under the administration of the League of Nations) voted the Unification with Germany in January 1935. A direct violation of the Treaty of Versailles was the increase of the Wehrmacht in March 1935, when Hitler didn't hesitate to announce that the German Army had not less than six hundred thousand soldiers, which was six times more than the limit set by the Treaty. With the help of the industry, the Nazis developed the Luftwaffe (German Air Forces) and also the Kriegsmarine (The German Navy). Another violation was the reoccupation of the Rhineland, which was until now a demilitarized zone. The Great Powers were watching passively as the Germans were breaking article after article of the Treaty of Versailles. In August 1936, Hitler ordered Hermann Göring to implement the Four Year Plan, which was supposed to prepare Germany for war in the next four years.

New Alliances

Unlike domestic politics where Hitler didn't trust any allies, he was aware that he would need to forge alliances for the war to come when it came to foreign policy. The first country Hitler felt he needed to approach was Italy, as he found a great source of inspiration in Benito Mussolini, the undisputed ruler of Italy. His attempt to seize power in 1923 was inspired by the "March on Rome," an action which led to naming Benito Mussolini the PrimeMinister of Italy. At that moment, Hitler and his Nazi followers were trying to seize power in Bavaria and then march on Berlin to challenge the government of that period. As this attempt failed, Hitler, being imprisoned for high treason, still had a lot of sympathy and respect for Il Duce (Benito Mussolini's nickname). He had wanted this alliance since the 1920s, but only when he had been appointed chancellor and auto proclaimed himself Führer could he make preparations for such alliances. Since the Führer was preparing for war, the first person to turn to was Mussolini, as he felt Il

Duce was his natural ally.

The two political leaders first met on October 25, 1936, when they created a strong bond and signed a treaty of alliance which was named "The Axis," after a quote from Benito Mussolini which stated that all the European countries will rotate on the "Rome-Berlin Axis." Just one month later, Germany signed an anti-communist pact with Japan, known as the Anti-Comintern Pact. Italy would join this alliance only in 1937. The Axis became a military alliance in 1939 and with Japan joining in 1940, it became the Tripartite Pact. Hitler and Mussolini had an intervention in the Spanish Civil War, both the leaders supporting General Franco. If Mussolini wanted to end the conflict with General Franco winning, Hitler just wanted to keep the war going. Italy supplied more than seventy thousand troops, while Germany provided a much smaller contribution.

The French wanted to limit the powers of a rising Germany, being aware of the military power it possessed. They were aware that Germany was going through a rearmament process, and they noticed the Germans occupying the Rhineland. Still, the French didn't want to engage in direct conflict, but instead, they forged an alliance with Soviet Russia, to decrease the Nazi threat for Central Europe. After this alliance, Hitler hated the French even more, as he thought they had endangered the whole of Europe by signing this treaty with the Soviets. Surprisingly, another country Hitler wanted to have as an ally was Great Britain. Since he was imprisoned, the Führer predicted an alliance with Great Britain, as it can be seen in his book, Mein Kampf. Although it was a country which criticized the Führer's violations of the Treaty of Versailles, Great Britain didn't take any action against Germany. Hitler felt like an alliance with the British could be possible, and he wasn't wrong. On June 18, 1935, the Anglo-German Naval Agreement was signed, a document which allowed the German Navy to grow in size, but limiting it to 35 percent of the British Navy. This was considered a great achievement by the Führer, as he thought that this would be the first step towards a German-British Alliance. However, by 1937, Hitler would have to renounce his plans for such an alliance, blaming it on the British leadership.

A Bigger Germany

Extending the Lebensraum was one of Hitler's greatest ambitions, as there were plenty of territories to conquer where the German people could live, while the native population was being eliminated or enslaved. The first step was to restore Germany's borders, as they were at the end of World War I before signing the Treaty of Versailles. The Saarland was already added to the German territory, and the Rhineland was under German control again. The easiest way for Germany to get bigger was to unite with Austria. On March 12, 1938, Hitler declared the unification of Austria with Germany or Anschluss. It was a process without any bloodshed, and Hitler had the opportunity to return to his homeland as a triumphant liberator. The Nazi army was greeted and cheered by the Austrian people.

The next on the list for Hitler was Czechoslovakia, where German ethnics mainly populated the Sudetenland region. He wasn't interested only in this region; he wanted the whole country. The Führer had a few meetings with some of the political leaders of the Sudeten German Party (which was the largest German ethnics party from this region) discussing a strategy to conquer Czechoslovakia. This party asked for increased autonomy from the Czechoslovakian government, but the real purpose was to have violent conflicts with the police. As the government agreed to all of the Sudeten German Party requests, a serious of violent clashes took place between the German ethnics acting on the command of the Sudeten German Party and the Czechoslovakian Police. This lead to the instauration of martial law in some of the Sudeten districts, which actually gave Hitler a reason to invade to protect the German ethnics from the Czechoslovakian authorities. Since Germany was relying on British oil, Hitler couldn't act immediately, although he ordered the Wehrmacht to prepare Fall Grün (Case Green) in April 1938. As the Great Powers were aware of the tensions in the Sudeten region, a peace conference was held which led to the annexation of Sudetenland by Germany. The conference was held in Munich on September 29, 1938, and the conference was attended by the prime minister of Great Britain (Neville Chamberlain), the prime minister of France (Edouard Daladier), and Benito Mussolini. The British prime minister was very pleased by the outcome of the peace conference, but he wasn't aware of Hitler's plans. The Führer met his enemies and this meeting only gave him more courage to pursue his military ambitions and foreign enemies, as he was convinced of their passivity and cowardliness to act. The German economy was going through a difficult period, as preparing for the war consumed a lot of resources and raw materials. Germany needed to increase exports to pay for raw materials required for its industry (it was a very high demand for iron in order to build all the elements of the German war machine: tanks, battleships, airplanes, guns, weapons, and ammunition).

However, he also thought that a neighboring country like Czechoslovakia might have some extra resources of iron and other raw materials, so he ordered the Wehrmacht to start the invasion of this country, by violating the Munich agreement. On March 15, the

German troops invaded and on March 16, Hitler announced from the Prague Castle that Bohemia and Moravia were under German Protectorate. Hitler took these two provinces for the German Lebensraum, as Bohemia and Moravia had belonged to the German Lebensraum for thousands of years. At this point, it was very clear to Great Britain and France that Hitler was not a man you could negotiate with, as his intentions were very clear, and he would not stop until he achieved his goals. The passive governments of these countries didn't take any action to stop Hitler from the very beginning, as they felt unprepared for a direct confrontation. However, if they were avoiding Germany, they would soon discover that the Wehrmacht would come to them.

Chapter 7
Leader of a War Machine

"I shall brew them a devil's drink"

*— Adolf Hitler reacting to the British "
guarantee" over the Polish independence.*

The Greater Germanic Reich

September 1, 1939, marked the beginning of World War II, a conflict
which would end the lives of millions, not just soldiers, but also
civilians. Not to mention the Holocaust which was the genocide of six
million European Jews, approximative two-thirds of the total Jewish
population in Europe. In pursuit of extending the Lebensraum, Hitler
was also determined to get back the land which belonged to East
Prussia, now being under Polish administration. By the end of summer
1939, Hitler was convinced he would have to act, being convinced that
Great Britain was his biggest enemy, and the invasion of Poland was
just one step to the final goal. August 1939 was the period of alliances
and pacts, like the Molotov-Ribbentrop Pact (a non-aggression
agreement between Germany and the Soviet Union signed between the
foreign ministers of these countries on August 23, 1939), but also the
Anglo-Polish Alliance of August 25, 1939. Hitler had reasons to
suspect that Mussolini would not honor the alliance he signed with
Nazi Germany, but he only delayed the invasion for a few days, as he
was planning to invade Poland on 25th August. The invasion of
Poland started on September 1, 1939, and this was the perfect

opportunity for Germany to prove its superiority on all possible levels.

Poland was no match for Germany, as the Luftwaffe was unchallenged in the skies, the Wehrmacht was able to advance easily, and the German battleships were able to bomb Polish ports within the range of their guns. The tactic was easy; the Wehrmacht would clear the way, and the SS troops would follow (an organization which had the initial purpose of protecting Hitler, but their activity diverged to intelligence activities and then running concentration camps). Their purpose in Poland was to Germanize the population, as they were looking for non-German and Jewish persons. Jews were often killed or eventually labeled. In Poland, the SS had conducted the most horrible crimes towards the Jewish community because they had in here the massive Jewish ghettos and also the horrific concentration camps. Hitler's official motivation for conquering Poland was to reclaim the land of East Prussia and to claim the free city of Danzig (Gdansk in Polish). Poland was an easy prize to win for Nazi Germany. However, it wasn't gained without consequences, as Great Britain and France finally declared war on Germany on September 3, 1939, but didn't launch an offensive on German troops or on Germany. Hitler could easily plan how to run the social purge in Poland, which would eventually lead to the deaths of millions of Jews. On April 9, 1940, Hitler invaded Denmark and Norway, and one month later, he launched his attack on France, Belgium, Luxembourg, and the Netherlands. Mussolini only joined forces on June 10, 1940, and on June 22, 1940, France surrendered and signed an armistice. Hitler had just implemented one of his visions, the creation of the Greater Germanic Reich, which united the racially pure nations of Scandinavian, Dutch and Flemish under German leadership. Just like in Poland, Hitler ran a Germanization strategy, so the SS targeted the

Jews in Denmark, Norway, Belgium, Luxembourg and the Netherlands. To increase his satisfaction, Hitler restored the same train coach in which the armistice of November 11, 1918, was signed. He invited the French officials to sign this time the surrender of France. The British troops were forced to return to England from the beaches of Dunkirk.

Hitler was very pleased with the outcome of the war so far, and he turned twelve of his generals into field marshals. It was because of their efforts France was conquered faster than Hitler expected, so the notion of Blitzkrieg was used to describe the invasion of France. The Luftwaffe could easily provide air support for the Wehrmacht and was unchallenged in the skies. However, things were about to change for the German Air Forces, because Hitler planned to attack Great Britain by air. The Battle of Britain was the clash between the British Royal Air Force and the German Luftwaffe, in which the German Luftwaffe suffered severe losses. Although it had more airplanes than the Royal Air Force, the Luftwaffe was outmaneuvered by very skilled and determined British pilots. The British fighter aircraft Supermarine Spitfire was superior to the German Messerschmitt BF 109, and this meant terrible loses for the Luftwaffe. The Battle of Britain was lost, Hitler suffering his first defeat of World War II. Since the German Navy couldn't stand a chance against the British Navy, a land invasion of Britain was not yet possible. Hitler settled for night air raids, bombing the most important cities in Great Britain. This strategy went on for months and amongst the cities where the Luftwaffe attacked were London, Coventry, and Plymouth.

The German forces were now stopped at the British Channel, as the Nazis couldn't go more to the West. Hitler would now have to concentrate on the Eastern part of Europe in order to conquer more land for the German people, but also to overthrow the Bolshevik regime of Joseph Stalin. As Hitler won Japan as an ally, other Eastern European countries joined him. Therefore, Hungary, Romania, and Bulgaria joined forces with Hitler to fight against the Soviet Union. By November 1940, Hitler was already preparing to attack the Soviet Union. In 1941, Hitler continued invading other countries like Yugoslavia, followed by Greece and Crete. Nazi troops were also supporting the Italians in Lybia (Northern Africa), and also the Iraqi rebel troops fighting against British forces. Therefore, German troops were present in Northern Africa, the Balkans, and also the Middle East as the conflict had spread more than the previous war.

Churchill made Hitler stop at the English Channel and also managed to close the Western Front in Europe. This can be considered a turning point of the War because it provided the first significant German losses in the battlefield and proved to the rest of the world that the Luftwaffe was not invincible. The RAF was the only thing standing between Hitler and his total victory over Western Europe. If the Germans would have won, that would probably mean the end of the war, but the war still continued for almost 5 more years. The Führer had to quit his claim to the British and focus on territories in Eastern Europe, lands which were so important for the Lebensraum. Another front was opened in Northern Africa, where the Nazis and the Italians were fighting Allied forces over control in this region. At this point, German troops were already fighting on three different continents, which was a war effort very hard to sustain, in terms of resources and manpower.

The Final Solution

The origin of anti-Semitic beliefs wasn't in the outcome of World War I, as the hatred towards Jews dates back a few centuries ago. In large parts of Europe, the Jewish community was amongst the wealthiest, as they were successful merchants who were richer and more powerful (in many cases) than the rest of the population. Back then, it was believed that Jews controlled the banks of Europe, and they also extended their influence over the politic class and large sectors of the economy. Although some may believe that Hitler was anti-Semitic from his teenage days, it was the period he spent in Vienna that fueled his hatred towards this nationality. In the former Austro-Hungarian Empire, he noticed the struggle of the German ethnics, as they were forced to live in the same state with eleven different nationalities. On top of that, the policy of the Empire was to favor the Slavic nations, so the German people were disadvantaged by this policy. However, the greatest threat to them was the Jewish community (according to all the German nationalists), as it had become so influent and powerful, that it was blocking the development of the German people (most of them working class, while the Jews were middle to high class).

It was the hate towards Jews and all the other ethnic groups of Vienna, which grew Hitler's contempt towards the Austro-Hungarian Empire and its capital. Being exposed to anti-Semitic rhetoric, he strongly believed that Jews were infiltrating the highest ranks of the political and financial positions. The surrender of Germany after World War I was also an extra reason to blame the Jews, as he believed that they were amongst the traitors responsible for the November 1918 armistice and the Treaty of Versailles. As a fervent German nationalist, Hitler swore to right the wrongs of that ceasefire armistice and the Treaty of Versailles, and also to punish severely the people he thought were responsible for the humiliation of Germany. The period after the war was marked by bloody social revolts, as several radical groups were trying to seize the power of Germany. Amongst them was the German Workers Party (DAP), which had a very radical approach towards Marxists and Jews. Hitler felt this was where he belonged, so he joined this party and in a very short period, he became its undisputed leader. Back then, politics was very combative, so in order to maintain security at the party's public meetings, or just to intimidate the political opponents, Hitler had to create a paramilitary group to act as the "iron fist" of the party. By this time, the German Workers' Party had become the National Socialist German Workers' Party, or in short, the Nazi party. This paramilitary group was called the SA and it served the Nazi party for many years, but soon Hitler lost his faith in this organization as it became very undisciplined, difficult to control, and far from being discrete. That's why Hitler created the SS, which was first intended as his personal guard, but in the years to come, this organization would play a much more important role.

The future of this organization was about to be shaped by Heinrich Himmler, who joined in 1925 and took over control of the SS in 1929. He reformed the organization and turned it into one of the most powerful and feared paramilitary groups in Germany. The role of the SS was minor at the beginning, being bodyguards for Hitler and other Nazi high leaders, but through them, Hitler saw a very useful group which could implement his visions of Nazi Germany. Therefore, the SS was trusted with very important missions like intelligence, security, surveillance, and spreading the terror throughout Germany and occupied territories. It rapidly increased, and by 1933 the organization had more than 209000 members. All their recruits were carefully selected, as they had to prove their Aryan background and to procure documents proving their ancestry all the way back to 1800 or 1750. A big part of the Nazi racial policy was stipulated by the Nuremberg Laws which were passed by the Reichstag on September 15, 1935. According to these laws, only those with German blood could be considered citizens of the Reich and anyone having three or more Jewish grandparents was considered a Jew. The marriage between a Jew and a person of German blood was strictly forbidden, as well as sexual relationships between Jews. Such laws also applied to the Romani community and the Black Germans.

The SS consisted of two separate entities, the Allgemeine SS and the Waffen SS. This first one was responsible for the implementation of Hitler's racial policy, while the other one was an elite fighting squad which joined the Wehrmacht during the war. A third element of the SS was later founded and was called the SS-Totenkopfverbände, which was the group responsible for running the concentration camps.

Heinrich Himmler soon became one of Hitler's closest henchmen, and the actions of the SS would severely affect the population of Europe. He was named the chief of police outside Prussia and the deputy of Himmler, Reinhard Heydrich was named the chief of Gestapo while he also had the position of Chief of the Security Service (SD). However, in order to "start the fire" against the Jewish community, Hitler needed a spark. On November 7, 1938, the German diplomat Ernst vom Rath was shot by a Polish Jew named Herschel Grynszpan in the German Embassy in Paris. Two days later, vom Rath died and gave the Nazi government the perfect opportunity to start a full-scale assault on Jews. On November 9 and 10, the SS, SA, and also German civilians carried out attacks on the Jews. More than 7500 Jewish stores were destroyed and over one thousand synagogues were damaged and burnt to the ground. Around ninety Jews were killed, and thirty thousand were sent to concentration camps in Dachau, Sachsenhausen, and Buchenwald. Most of the Jews sent to these camps were eventually released, but around two thousand of them were still kept in the camps. This whole operation was known as the Kristallnacht, and even though it didn't lead to countless deaths, it marked the end of the Jewish public activities and culture. For some Jews, this was the clear signal that it was time to leave Germany.

In 1939, all the police and security service was concentrated into one organization which was called the Reich Main Security Office, which was lead by the same Reinhard Heydrich. Hitler saw in Himmler the right man to enforce his racial policy, as he shared the same views towards Jews and other inferior ethnic groups. Himmler and his deputy (Heydrich) unleashed the genocide of at least six million Jews and more than 10 million other deaths in different ethnic groups like Soviets, Romani, Serbs, gay men and many more.

In the invasions campaign, wherever the Wehrmacht would go, the SS would follow, starting the ethnic cleansing policy. In the beginning, they shot the "socially impure" elements of the population, but as they ran into large numbers of Jews, they decided to label and force them to live in ghettos after being stripped of all their possessions. As the number of captured Jews was growing very fast, the SS would have to implement a very effective solution to exterminate the Jews. This was why the concentration camps appeared as part of Operation Reinhard (named after Himmler's deputy, who was the mastermind behind this process). There were major concentration camps, most of them being in Poland. These were Auschwitz, Belzec, Chelmno, Majdanek, Maly Trostinets, Sobibor, and Treblinka. In these camps, the Nazis would unleash terror on the Jews, as they were forced to work in inhumane condition until they were exhausted and eventually sent to large chambers where they were killed using toxic gas like Zyklon-B, Hydrogen cyanide, and prussic gas.

Most of the Jews killed by these concentration camps were from Poland (around 2.1 million), Soviet Union (approximately the same number), and Hungary (more than half a million Jews). The deadliest concentration camps were Auschwitz, Treblinka, and Belzec with more than 1.1 million, 870 thousand and 600 thousand Jews killed. In the occupied territories, some of the Jews and other ethnic groups didn't make it to concentration camps, as they were shot on the spot. Tens of thousands were killed this way, but in other situations, the Nazis had orders to starve the local population and only provide food and supplies to the Germans. Reinhard Heydrich was assassinated in 1942 by a group of Czech partisans, but this didn't change the plans of exterminating the Jews and other ethnic groups. By summer 1943, it was becoming very clear that the Germans would lose the war. However, this didn't stop the killing. Josef Mengele, an SS officer, but also a physician at Auschwitz, performed deadly human experiments on Jews. This is why he received the nickname "Angel of Death."

Overall, the SS was responsible for the killing of almost six million Jews, seven million Soviets (of which 1.3 million were Soviets Jews), two to three million Soviet prisoners, 1.8-1.9 million Poles, between 300 thousand to 500 thousand Serbs, around 200 thousand to 220 thousand Romani. They showed no mercy to the disabled, gay men, and also Jehovah's Witnesses, by killing many of them.

Any other tragedy in human history can hardly match with the genocide of the Jewish people and also other ethnic groups. It massively depopulated the regions of Central and Eastern Europe, to create space for the German colonizing population. Approximately two-thirds of the Jewish population in Europe was annihilated, the other third managed to escape the wrath of the Nazi regime. After the war, many Jews settled in what is known today as Israel, a new state which started to expand in a few years after the war, causing massive tensions and conflicts with some Arab states. Middle East was as hostile to the Jews as Nazi Germany was during World War II, but the Holocaust is considered by any Jew the biggest tragedy in all their history.

Although mostly everyone on the planet knows about the Holocaust, anti-Semitism didn't die at the end of World War II and anti-Semitic beliefs are still present, especially in times like economic crises.

The Turning Point

Hitler always had the ambition of destroying the Soviet Union and wiping out the communist ideology, as he hated Marxists almost as much as he hated Jews. On top of that, he was convinced that the rise of Communism was financed by wealthy Jewish bankers, in the attempt to destroy the Russian Empire, but it was also a threat for entire Europe. Although he didn't attack the Soviet Union repeatedly as he was focusing on destroying the Western Great Powers. Once he realized that Great Britain couldn't be invaded, he turned his attention towards the East where there was plenty of lands for German people to settle and also some Slavic nations he hated so much, but most of all, many Jews. As he considered them subhumans, Hitler was determined to wipe out these nations from the face of Europe. It happened with the conquest of Yugoslavia and Ukraine, two Slavic countries, where Hitler wanted to exterminate a large amount of the native population, not just the Jews. At this point, the Führer had now more allies, such as Hungary, Romania, and Bulgaria and the Romanian oil was not fueling the German war machine. The Hungarian, Romanian and Bulgarian Army joined with the Germans as it was very clear that Hitler was planning to invade the Soviet Union.

On June 22, 1941, Hitler launched the offensive on the Soviet Union, conquering countries like the Baltic Republics, Belarus and West Ukraine. The invasion was planned to take place on three fronts, a western one towards Leningrad (modern-day Sankt Petersburg), a central one towards Moscow and a southern one through Kiev. The plan was to attack Moscow from three different sides, causing the surrender of the Soviets. However, at this point, Hitler was somehow convinced that he was a great tactician and very often he disagreed with his generals what strategy to adopt. After advancing about five hundred kilometers into enemy territory, the Germans and the Russians finally clashed at the Battle of Smolensk (Soviet resistance didn't stop the German advance). This was the first major victory of the Germans on the Eastern front, but it was also followed by poor decisions coming from Hitler. The Führer had ordered the Centre Army Group to stop its advance and to aid the German troops on the other flanks, Western and Southern, as Hitler wanted to conquer Leningrad and Kiev. The Centre Army Group was just 400 km outside Moscow and the order to stop the advance wasn't an order that the generals agreed with, so there was a crisis amongst the ranks of German military leadership. This gave the perfect opportunity for the Soviet troops to mobilize and prepare intensively for the defense of Moscow. On the Eastern front, this decision was one of Hitler's major mistakes. The advance was only continued in October 1941, but the massive invasion and attack on Moscow from three sides was not going to happen. The weather conditions significantly got worse as German tanks were being stuck in the mud, and as they advanced deeper into the enemy territory, they were also starting to run out of supplies. Winter was Hitler's biggest problem, as the German soldiers or tanks were not equipped for such harsh conditions. The full-scale invasion on Moscow could have meant the end of the war with a Nazi victory. For the Allies, it was crucial for Hitler to be defeated at Moscow.

The attack on Moscow, called Operation Typhoon ended very badly for the Germans, as the attack itself failed. Stalin mobilized troops from the Siberian and Far Eastern territories to defend the capital and also created three defensive zones outside Moscow, which managed to stop the Germans from going further. They also prepared a counter-offensive which succeeded in pushing Hitler's troops back to the towns of Oryol, Vyazma, and Vitebsk. The Soviet troops were very close to surrounding the three German armies. The Führer took matters into his own hands and appointed himself as the supreme commander of German military forces. This was a catastrophic blow to the Wehrmacht as it would not obtain any important victory from now on. The end of 1942 marked the turning point of World War II when Nazi troops were losing battle after battle.

In their attempts to control Egypt and the Suez canal, the Germans were defeated by the British at El Alamein (twice) and Alam el Halfa, preventing the Italian-German troops moving forward into Egypt and taking control of the Suez Canal. However, it all culminated with the Battle of Stalingrad from August 1942 to February 1943. The offensive of Stalingrad was going according to plan, the Luftwaffe successfully bombing the city and the Wehrmacht was able to push out the Soviet soldiers. However, the Soviet forces started Operation

Uranus, with the strategy to flank the Axis forces by targeting the weaker Romanian and Hungarian armies. The strategy was successful, as the Soviet forces managed to surrender the German troops in an attempt to cut off their supply chain. The operation nearly wiped out the entire German 6th Army, as the Axis troops suffered severe losses in what was the bloodiest battle of the war. Almost half a million soldier lives were lost and more than six hundred thousand soldiers were wounded or ill. Hitler refused to yield control of the city, so he ordered the 6th Army to stand its ground and keep Stalingrad under German control. By February 1943, the Axis troops were running out of supplies, so they had to surrender to the Soviet Army. More than 265 thousand soldiers surrendered and the Russian forces took them as prisoners. This loss was a devastating blow to the Axis forces, losing countless lives, but also many tanks, airplanes, and guns. The Wehrmacht already lost many soldiers, but the German propaganda successfully convinced the people of Germany to volunteer for the war. Such forces lacked the discipline and training for the war, so they were not very helpful for the Führer.

The Battle of Stalingrad was considered to be the turning point of World War II, as it gave a devastating blow to the German forces. From then on the Wehrmacht fought from a position of retreat and didn't even dream of getting close to Moscow. It simply marked the beginning of the end for the German troops, as it signaled the Allied forces to engage the Nazis and open up different fronts, like the one in Italy and eventually to reopen the Western front with the Normandy campaign (or Operation Overlord). The Axis troops had to change tactics, from a full-scale offensive to vigorously defensive.

Chapter 8
Path to Ruin

"I know as well as you, Duce, how difficult it is to take historical decisions, but I am not certain that after my death another will be found with the necessary force of will...I consider that is by the grace of Providence that I have been chosen to lead my people in such a war."

– Adolf Hitler to Benito Mussolini in one of his letters to the Italian leader

Assassination Attempts

By seizing all the power for himself, Hitler "won" a few enemies, some of them who wanted him dead. Hitler was aware of this, so he entrusted Nazi members to create paramilitary organizations which would serve as protection for him or other Nazi high leaders. Most of the assassination attempts were plotted by German citizens, as Jews or another ethnic group could barely get close to the Führer. In the 1920s Hitler was almost completely unknown outside Bavaria, and his SA could protect him from any political opponent within this region. He was still a small figure and just an agitator, so there aren't any records of assassination attempts on him during that period. As he was becoming one of the most important persons of the political scene in Germany, he had opponents within other parties, but also the Nazi party itself. However, none of them was as radical as Hitler, so they never posed a threat to his life. This was about to change from 1932 since he became the leader of the most powerful party in Germany.

Since that year, there were several attempts to kill Hitler, most of them being discovered in time by the SS leaders, so the Führer remained alive to the final days of World War II.

There were not less than forty-two attempts to assassinate Hitler, since 1932 until the final attempt in July 1944. Some of the attempts were carried out by former fighters in the Freikorps (Beppo Römer who had several attempts), a German carpenter (Johann Georg Elser), a German diplomat (Erich Kordt), a German Jew (Helmut Hirsch), Polish officers, and a mental patient. However, the most dangerous attempts on Hitler's life were carried out by officers of the German Army. Most of these German officers were convinced that Hitler was leading the country to ruin, and they felt it was their patriotic duty to assassinate the Führer and take control over Germany to discuss with the Allies on different terms. Even though the Führer gave them medals and ranks, these officers felt they were stripped of power, as the Führer was deciding the war strategy instead of them. Perhaps they would have accepted this if Hitler had experience in acting as an officer within the German Army, but they were aware that Hitler was a former dispatch runner who didn't fight in World War I and most of all didn't know anything about military strategy. Hitler's war strategy led to countless deaths within the Wehrmacht as many of his ambitions weren't sustainable on the front.

The first attempt to kill Hitler by army officers was planned in September 1938, when Hitler was planning to invade Czechoslovakia. General Major Hans Oster and other officers plotted to arrest or kill Hitler, in case he invaded Czechoslovakia. There were planning to seize power and replace Hitler with the exiled Emperor Wilhelm II. As the Munich peace conference just offered the Sudetenland to Germany, this plan didn't take place. However, some of the officers were involved in future plots against Hitler. As the tide of the war was turning and now the odds were against the German Army, the plots were a lot more frequent. By this time, Hitler already lost the Battle of Moscow and the Battle of Stalingrad due to his war strategy, and high-ranking officers conspired to replace and assassinate the Führer. Hitler planned a visit in Ukraine to inspect the Army Detachment Kempf, which meant that this was the perfect opportunity for generals like Hubert Lanz, Hans Speidel, and Hyazinth Graf Strachwitz to surround the Führer and his escort with the tanks, to arrest or eventually kill Hitler and the SS guards. For unknown reasons, the visit was canceled.

Another attempt was on March 13, 1943, when Hitler visited the Army Group Center in Smolensk. Major Georg von Boeselager planned to intercept and kill the Führer (with the help of other officers) on his way from the airport to the base, but a massive force of SS troops guarded Hitler, so he didn't carry out the plan. Henning von Tresckow and Boeselager wanted to assassinate Hitler during lunchtime, but they dropped the plan since Himmler was not present with Hitler. Field Marshall Günther von Kluge knew about this plan but didn't want to take part in it. When the Führer returned to the aircraft, Tresckow gave to an officer from Hitler's escort a bomb camouflaged as a liqueur. The bomb was supposed to explode on the return flight over Poland, but the package was placed in the hold of the airplane and instead of exploding, it froze causing the ignition mechanism to fail. Realizing the failure of this attempt, a soldier named Fabian von Schlabrendorff flew to Germany to recover the suitcase before it was discovered. There were other attempts of German officers to assassinate Hitler, but none was as close as the 20th July plot, also named Operations Valkyrie. The key role in this plot was played by

Colonel Claus von Stauffenberg, a young German officer who fought in the invasion of Poland and the Soviet Union, and also in Northern Africa. Alongside General Friedrich Olbricht and Major General Henning von Tresckow, he planned to kill Hitler, arrest the Nazi leaders and disarm the SS troops. The plan was to introduce a bomb into the Wolf's Lair (Hitler's Hidden Command Center) in order to assassinate him and also to mobilize the German Reserve Army to seize power. Colonel von Stauffenberg successfully introduced the suitcase into the Command Center. However, the attempt didn't kill the Führer. There was a massive explosion, but Hitler survived, and all the officers who conspired to kill him were arrested for high treason (and eventually killed).

Territory Loss

For Germany, the war was lost after the Battle of Moscow and the Battle of Stalingrad. Hitler lost a lot of resources on the Eastern Front, including countless human casualties. Too many good soldiers lost their lives during these battles of the Eastern front, and the Führer could only replace them with civilians. Not to mention how many tanks and artillery weapons were lost during the battles of the Eastern front. Germany couldn't keep up with the losses, as the industry in Germany couldn't provide that many tanks, airplanes, guns, rifles, or machine guns. As for the civilian volunteers, many of them were too young or too old, so they weren't very helpful for Hitler. Under these circumstances, the Wehrmacht had to run a defensive war, as they no longer had support from the Luftwaffe and didn't have the resources to run a full-scale offensive. They had to retreat from Russia, Ukraine, and the Baltic states, as they couldn't face the Soviet troops.

However, the German Army would make one big last stand on the Eastern front in the Battle of Kursk. This was the biggest tank battle in all history, with Germany on one side having half a million men, 10 thousand guns and mortars, 2700 tanks and around 2500 planes. The Soviet Union was even better equipped, having 1.3 million soldiers, more than 20 thousand guns and mortars, around 3600 tanks and approximately 2650 planes. In addition to that, they also had half a million men and another 1500 tanks as reserves. Even though the Russians outnumbered the Germans, and they had more military equipment, the losses were a lot greater on the Russian side. The new Tiger tank used by the Germans proved to be very effective in this battle, but still, it couldn't make a decisive difference, so the Soviets won the battle although paying a very high cost. The Wehrmacht never recovered from this devastating blow which was the war on the Eastern Front, as they couldn't replace all the lost manpower and armor. At this point, the Nazis were forced to retreat also on other fronts, not just the Eastern one. They were no longer present in Northern Africa and they had to fight on Italian soil, as the Allies were advancing towards Rome. In the Soviet Union, the Russian troops were chasing out the German forces, and they were following them towards Germany through Ukraine, the Baltic States, and Poland.

Since the Allies couldn't march on Germany from Italy (because of the Alps), they had to re-open the Western front. On June 6, 1944, the Allies landed in Normandy in a very brave attempt to advance towards Germany. A total of 156 thousand British, American, and Canadian troops landed on the beaches of Normandy. The Nazis had a fierce resistance, but the allies prevailed and secured the position in Normandy. After just one week, the beaches of Normandy were flooded with more than 326 thousand troops, 100 thousand tons of equipment and more than 50 thousand vehicles. With enemies closing on them from the East and also from the West, the German Army had to fight to protect their homeland, as the Allies were already bombing German cities.

At the beginning of the invasion of Soviet Russia, Nazi Germany was controlling most of continental Europe. However, now the situation had dramatically changed. Being out of manpower and armor, the Wehrmacht couldn't withstand much longer, so in about eleven months from the Normandy Invasion, the war would be over with the German Army defeat.

The Final Days

By the end of 1944, the Soviet Army and the Allied troops were already marching into Germany. As he couldn't launch a massive offensive on both armies, he decided to attack the Allied troops, as he considered that the Red Army was far stronger. Thus, on 16th December 1944, Hitler ordered the Ardennes Offensive, a desperate attempt to push the Allies back. The Reserve Army mobilized for this operation had some brief temporary successes, but the Allies fought back and continued their advance into Germany. By January 1945, a large part of Germany was already in ruins, and Hitler had to take even more desperate measures. He didn't want the German industry to fall into the Allies hands, so he ordered the destruction of any industrial facilities throughout Germany. Albert Speer, who in the last years served as Minister for Armaments, was entrusted with this task, but he didn't carry on with this task, secretly disobeying Hitler's orders. The death of the American President Roosevelt had given Hitler hopes for a peace negotiation with the US and Great Britain. However, this didn't happen as the allies didn't want to negotiate with him.

There is a theory that high ranking Nazi leaders managed to escape from Berlin (while it was bombed and attacked by the Soviet troops) and fled to South America (via Italy). It looked like the countries of this continent were the ideal place for Nazi members to hide from justice, as they knew that the Allies would not show them any mercy. There is also a theory that Hitler managed to escape and fled to South America, but most historians would disagree with it. In the last days of the war, Hitler was hiding in his bunker in Berlin, just waiting for the inevitable. On April 20, 1945, Hitler made his last public appearance in the garden of the Reich Chancellery. He made the last preparations for the defense of Berlin, placing the Army Group Vistula outside Berlin to prevent the Red Army advance and also had a group of under-equipped soldiers placed under the command of Felix Steiner, the commander of the Waffen SS. On April 21, 1945, the Soviet Army had destroyed every defense of the German Army and was preparing for a siege of Berlin. Just two days later, they completely surrounded the German capital and meticulously bombed Berlin, advancing street by street and crushing any German resistance.

Goebbels incited the residents of Berlin to defend their city, but they were no match for the Red Army. In all this time, Göring was at Bertechsgaden in the Bavarian Alps, far from the bombings of Berlin and waiting to assume leadership. He sent a telegram to the Führer providing arguments that he should be become the leader, as the Führer was surrounded in Berlin. He also left a deadline for the Führer, Göring considering that if Hitler failed to reply it was because he was incapacitated. On April 28, Hitler discovered that Himmler had fled Berlin on April 20, and he was planning to surrender and negotiate with the Allies. The Führer ordered the arrest of Himmler and in his will, he removed Göring of all his government positions. He soon found out about Mussolini's execution, and he felt more determined to avoid capture at all costs. Grand Admiral Karl Dönitz was appointed the head of state, while Joseph Goebbels was named chancellor.

Only the closest Nazi members were staying in the bunker with Hitler, as they wanted to be by his side in the final hours of the 3rd German Reich. As a family friend, Goebbels brought his whole family into the bunker. So Magda Goebbels with all their six children was also in the bunker. They couldn't accept the German defeat and they didn't want to live in a world without Hitler, so they were all prepared to die like their Führer.

In the last days Hitler spent in the bunker, he married his mistress, Eva Braun at the end of April and just forty hours later, Hitler shot himself while his wife bit into a cyanide capsule. The bodies were taken out by SS officers, placed in a bomb crater and burnt. On May 2, 1945, Berlin surrendered, so the Soviet troops were able to go into the Reich Chancellery and also into the back garden where they found the bunker. The remains of Hitler and Eva Braun were completely burnt by the time the Russian soldiers found them, and nobody was able to identify Hitler's body. A lower jaw with dental work on it could have been identified as Hitler's remain.

The end... almost!

Reviews are not easy to come by.

As an independent author with a tiny marketing budget, I rely on readers, like you, to leave a short review on Amazon.

Even if it's just a sentence or two!

So if you enjoyed the book, please...

>> Click here to leave a brief review on Amazon.

https://www.amazon.com/review/create-review?asin=XXXXXXXXX

I am very appreciative for your review as it truly makes a difference.

Thank you from the bottom of my heart for purchasing this book and reading it to the end.

Final Thoughts

Without any doubt, Hitler was the biggest threat to not only the Jewish community of the twentieth century, but also the Slavic ethnics and communists of Eastern Europe. His actions to ensure the Lebensraum for the German people involved conquering new countries and eliminating (or enslaving) the natives. He held a grudge against communists, Jews, Slavic populations and Romani ethnics, as Hitler considered these groups as subspecies or subhumans. In his views, only the Germans, Scandinavian population, the Dutch and the Flemish were considered Aryan, the superior race, as all the other nationalities and ethnic groups would have to submit to the will of the Aryan race.

Hitler's purge on the inferior nations and ethnic groups was a racial cleansing from which not less than seventeen million lives were lost. Approximately two-thirds of the Jewish population in Europe was killed, but Hitler also killed almost one million Poles, between two and three million Soviet prisoners, around half a million Serbs. When it comes to the Romani population, official numbers indicate between 200 thousand and 220 thousand, but some historians would disagree and would estimate between half a million and 1.5 million deaths. The purge on all these ethnic groups is probably what motivated the Allied troops to defeat the Nazis and their allies. If Hitler had won the Battle of Moscow, probably the war would have ended with Hitler having control over most of continental Europe. However, just like Napoleon in 1812, Hitler was defeated, and he failed to conquer Moscow and to continue the ethnic purge over the population of the Soviet Union.

The Russian invasion or Operation Barbarossa as it was officially named proved to be a campaign with devastating results for the German Army, a campaign which led to its defeat. There were too many casualties amongst the German Army and too many resources were lost within this conflict. It was a clear example that not even the mighty Wehrmacht could overcome the weather and conquer Russia, as the German tanks were not functional in the Russian mud or cold, and the German soldiers were not used to fight in extremely low temperatures. Not to mention that food supplies were very difficult to get. Most historians would agree that the Battle of Stalingrad was the turning point of this war when the Axis forces were surrounded and defeated by the Soviet troops. In a battle that lasted for a few months, the German 6th Army was almost completely annihilated by the Soviet forces who managed to cut off their supplies. It was the bloodiest battle in this war, causing the German Army a devastating blow from which it did not recover. From this point, the German Army implemented a defensive strategy, as they didn't have any more resources to run a full-scale offensive to win the war. The Soviet Army was the one to bring Berlin to ruin and to end the war by causing the Nazis to surrender and Hitler to commit suicide in the bunker just below Berlin. The Führer wanted to avoid at any cost the humiliation of captivity, after hearing of Mussolini's execution. He didn't want to answer for his crimes against Jews and all the other ethnic groups which suffered from his racial cleansing.

If Hitler couldn't have been caught to stand before a judge and be trialed, other important Nazi leaders were captured, and they faced justice in the Nuremberg trials. Some of the most important figures which were trialed were Hermann Göring, Rudolf Hess, Karl Dönitz, Albert Speer, and Julius Streicher. As some of the fanatic Nazi members escaped to South America, most of them didn't face any trial, as the political regime of these countries protected them. The Jewish Mossad managed to capture Alfred Eichmann (one of the key figures of the Holocaust) and bring him for trial in Israel.

World War II left Europe in ruins, as major parts of Germany, France, and Eastern Europe were bombed and destroyed. No other conflict in history has generated such mass destruction and loss of lives. The European countries continued to suffer after the war, as they were trying to rebuild their cities and their economy. It took an awful amount of time for all these countries to recover economically and demographically, but they managed to rise again in a period of peace and prosperity. Organizations like the UN, NATO and the modern day European Union were designed to assure peace and prosperity in Europe and around the world. Unfortunately, the fall of Nazi Germany didn't mean the death of this ideology, as nowadays it can be found in newer forms of hatred and radicalism called Neo-Nazi organizations. To understand this movement we first need to find its roots and discover the causes of this movement, in order to prevent racial tensions from escalating and turning into conflicts which may lead to deaths. Adolf Hitler can never be considered a role model, but he can be an anti-model, the type of character which has to be studied to discover his flaws. To learn from mistakes (in this case Hitler's mistakes) is the best way to gather knowledge and only by looking in the past, we can shape a brighter and more peaceful future.

DOWNLOAD YOUR FREE GIFT BELOW:

These 14 New Habits Will Double Your Income, from Today

An Easy Cheat Sheet to Adopting 14 Powerful Success Habits:

Stop Procrastinating and Start Earning with Intent Now!

Are Your Bad Habits Keeping You from the Life You Want?

Mine definitely were, but then I dedicated myself to *new habits* – and everything changed!

Most people get stuck in same old routines. We eat the same breakfast, we talk to the same people. Human beings are creatures of habit, and it locks us into negative cycles we don't even know are there.

Like me, you've had enough of the same-old, same-old. It's time for change!

This guide gives you the 14 most high impact habits that helped me double my income nearly instantly, when I set out on this journey. I will help you change, and I'll make it stick!

This FREE Cheat Sheet contains:

- Daily success habits that the most successful people in the world live by

- Common, but little-known habits that will surprise you

- Details on what Stephen Covey, Oprah Winfrey, Elon Musk, Bill Gates and Albert Einstein did that you aren't doing to maximize your earning potential

- Tips on how to overcome habit fatigue

- The reality of adopting difficult, challenging habits and the rewards that result

Scroll below and click the link to claim **your cheat sheet!**

It's tough to admit that you're doing it wrong. I went through it, and it sucks. After that I was free to change however necessary, to meet my goals. I want you to know that change is waiting for you. This guide is so easy to follow, and if you put it to work in your life – you will double your income.

Adopt these habits, and change your life.

CLICK HERE!!

Check Out Our Other AMAZING Titles!

Book 1: <u>Celtic Myths and Legend Stories</u>

<u>Gods, Men, and Stories of Celtic Legends</u>

Local Celtic Gods

The life and passion of a person leave an imprint on the ether of a place. Love does not remain within the heart, it flows out to build secret tabernacles in a landscape.

- John O'Donohue

While some gods were more popular than others, you must remember that the Celts were a diverse group of people. Many gods were worshipped in other forms and names, which created the impression that the Celts had an innumerable number of gods they worshipped.

While the number of their gods is high, a lot of inflation occurs thanks to each tribe worshipping a differently named god who is essentially the same deity. In this chapter, we're going to look at some of the more common local Celtic gods who had a major influence on their cultures.

Irish Gods

Ireland provides a large number of Celtic gods simply because their records survived more than others. Continental Europe constantly saw major upheavals, and as such, any records from Northern France or Spain were lost. This is why in the previous chapter, all of the gods referred to were from Ireland, Scotland, or England.

Irish gods provide us with the best background information on how other Celtic tribes worshipped their equivalent gods, so it's of extreme value to examine them and get to know them better.

Aine

Aine is one of Ireland's premier fairy queens and is a goddess associated with the seasons and wealth and prosperity. She is generally associated with the sun and is usually represented by a red mare. While she may not be worshipped in huge numbers today, records indicate that as recently as 1879, the locals around the hill of Knockainey (named after Aine) were conducting rites honoring her (Celticlife, n.d.).

Aine's name could mean anything from joy, splendor, to happiness, and these indicate the sort of feelings she inspired.

Manannan Mac Lir

Also known as Manann, this god is technically not isolated to Ireland. He was worshipped in many forms across the channel as well, but he appears the most in Irish tales. He was a god associated with the seas, and his full name translates as Manann, son of the sea (Celticlife, n.d.).

His boat is named Scuabtuinne, which is really a chariot that is drawn across the waves by the horse Aonbharr. He wields a sword named Fragarach as well as a cloak of invisibility. He is also a guardian and guide to the Otherworld. All in all, there are a ton of stories about him and adventures recorded about him.

Angus Og

Also referred to as Aengus or Angus the younger, he is the son of the Dagda and Boann. Angus is the god of love and is most associated with youth and poetic inspiration. Angus was the result of an affair between the Dagda and Boann. To hide her pregnancy, Boann made the sun stand still for nine months and thus gestated the boy Angus in a single day.

Once he was born, he realized that his father had already divided all of his lands between his children and nothing was left for Angus. Despite this, he met his father and asked him whether he could live in his home for "a night and a day." Now, the Irish language has no indefinite article ("a"), so in effect, the Dagda permitted his son to live in his home "night and day." Thus, Angus ended up getting his own home (Celticlife, n.d.).

An alternate version of this story has the Dagda advising Angus of this method in order to trick Elcmar, the husband of Boann, from his property.

Boann

The river Boyne was anointed as a goddess and this entity was Boann. Legend has it that a woman named Boann once approached a sacred well which was the source of all knowledge. Now, everyone except for the god of water, Nechtan, was forbidden from approaching this well. As punishment for her crime, the waters of the well swelled and enveloped her, and she either drowned or outran the current.

Thus, the river Boann or Boyne was born.

Bran the Blessed

Bran technically belongs to both Welsh and Irish culture. Legend has it that he was a giant and ruler of Wales and is approached by the king of Ireland for his sister Branwen's hand in marriage in order to form an alliance between the two islands. While Bran agrees, unfortunately, a half-brother of theirs is angered at his not being consulted. As a result, he mutilates the horses of the Irish king.

The marriage still goes ahead despite this, but the insult rankles among the Irish. This results in Branwen being mistreated, and she gets the word out to her brothers. The brothers prepare for war and eventually reach Ireland. They set a trap for the Irish king, but this backfires and results in a bloody battle. The half-brother realizes that the Irish are resurrecting their dead using a cauldron and jumps into it and destroys it from the inside, thus killing himself.

Eventually, Bran's head is severed from his body, though it regains consciousness and keeps the six other survivors occupied. Eventually, the head is buried in what is considered to be the current location of the Tower of London and points towards France in order to deter an invasion. I mean, the Irish are schemers, but the French are the real villains in all of this, so this is completely justified.

Gallic Gods

I've been confining myself to Britain thus far in this book, but now it's time to crossover into continental Europe and visit the Gauls. The Gauls formed many tribes within themselves, and each tribe had its own pantheon of gods. However, there were some common gods who made an appearance.

Some of these gods possessed the same characteristics as the major gods listed in the previous chapter. While they might not be known by the same names, there is no denying the similarities. Also, Gallic gods take a lot of inspiration from their Greek counterparts thanks to the influence of Rome and ancient Greece on continental Europe.

Esus

Esus is one of the most revered gods in Gallic culture. There are more inscriptions of him than every other god combined. His worship was so prevalent that even Julius Caesar is said to have noticed his importance among his enemies. A close friend of Esus was Cernunnos, and they are often depicted together (Celticlife, n.d.).

Esus, or Mercury, as he was known in Roman myth, is said the be the son of Maia, a Titan, and Jupiter. The Romans never paired him up with anyone, but the Gauls consider Rosmerta to be his companion, and they are often shown together. Esus is the inventor of all arts, the guardian of travelers, and is the god who presides over all aspects of commerce and grain.

Rosmerta

Rosmerta, who was mostly depicted with Mercury/Esus, is a fertility goddess and is alternatively seen carrying a basket of fruit or a two-headed axe. As the wife of Esus, she was quite popular in Gaul and was associated with the earth (Maia). In addition to this, she was also associated with abundance.

Belenos

Belenos was a popular deity and was alternatively called Belenus. He was particularly popular in Switzerland and Gaul. Given that his name translates to "bright one," he was likely associated with the sun or fire, which makes him the equivalent of Apollo to the Romans.

The Irish associated him with Bile/Beli, who happened to be the god of the underworld as well. Although the ancient Celts didn't have a notion of hell, the underworld was still a place best avoided. These contradicting associations likely point to a misunderstanding in our translation of ancient texts or in perhaps the way the Romans recorded information. As such, this is all we know as of now.

Arduinna

Arduinna, who the Romans associated with Artemis from Greek myth, is the goddess of hunting and is depicted riding the back of a wild boar. She was extremely popular in parts of Gaul and modern-day Belgium, especially among tribes in the Ardennes region.

Book 2: <u>Norse Mythology</u>

<u>To the Gates of Valhalla - A Journey Through the Twisted Mythology of the Norse Peoples</u>

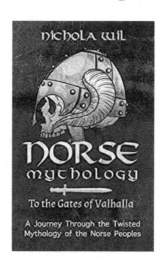

The End: Ragnarok

"Brothers will fight and kill each other, sisters' children will defile kinship. It is harsh in the world, whoredom rife —an axe age, a sword age —shields are riven— a wind age, a wolf age— before the world goes headlong. No man will have mercy on another."

Dronke (1997:19)

From chaos, the world began until the gods were born of that very strife. The gods did their very best to create and sustain order in the universe, but this was very trying and required a lot of energy. As the gods themselves did not have infinite power, it was inevitable that the order they required and abided by being ultimately subsumed into the vacuum of the chaos, thus completing the circle of life for Norse gods. Their beginning required their ending, and the ending was written in their genesis; so it can be said that the Norse gods never had a chance, and by extension, neither did the Viking people.

That said, it was the weather's fault, ultimately. It was the Twilight of the Gods, known as Ragnarokkr. The Fates had foretold that a Great Winter was on its way, the Fimblvetr, and it would be the worst that the world had ever seen. The Vikings were a northern people, already accustomed to extreme temperatures, biting gales, and suffocating drifts of omnipresent winter snow. The Fimblvetr was the winter to outrank all others. It would last for the span of three normal winters, with no intervening summers to warm the cold and allow time for harvest. The stories spun by the Fates of resulting hunger, of imminent strife, as man began to fight his brethren for food and base survival, chilled the Viking peoples to the bone.

The Fates looked upward, to the void of the sky, and prophesied that the stars would fall out of the night. The trees and the mountains were to fall to the ground. The wolves which had been restrained from ravishing the world would be released. The serpent slithering at the bottoms of the seas would surface, spilling the oceans over the land and hissing at all who stood in his way.

Amid all this chaos, a mighty ship which had been moored for all eternity, until the end of things, would sail. This ship was known as Naglfar, the Nail Ship, as it was formed of fingernails and toenails gleaned from corpses.

Naglfar needed a captain, and while hell broke loose over Earth, Loki quietly broke free of the chains the gods had forced upon him to pilot the Nail Ship.

The wolf Fenrir was to rove over the dying world, eating all who stood in his way. The sea-serpent poisoned all land, sea, and sky with his venom.

Ymir's skull, forming the sky since the beginning of the world, would crack in half. Flying through the break would come the fire and ice gods from the elemental lands of Muspelheim and Niflheim, and led by a leader with a flaming sword they would march on Asgard, the heavenly home of the gods. However, they were likewise fated to fail in their mission: the bridge leading to Asgard was foretold to bend and break beneath the unlucky usurpers.

Even though they were spared this particular onslaught, the gods were aware of the story of their own downfall. They would read the signs -- they'd see the sea-serpent and the hungry wolf ravaging Earth; they'd see Naglfar, and they would know that Loki had escaped. Odin, the king of the gods, would consult with his counsel, even though they knew they were doomed. As the Vikings themselves would do, even if their defeat was assured, the gods prepared for battle. They strapped on their armor and polished their swords, then set sail for Vigridr, the "Plain Where the Battle was to Surge."

Odin would fight the wolf Fenrir and be eaten. To avenge him, Odin's son Vidar would step into battle, sneering at the wolf, brandishing his sword, kicking his feet. This last was more effective than it might have otherwise sounded, and Vidar knew it: he would be wearing a shoe crafted for the final battle, a shoe which had been carefully cobbled from every piece of leather which had ever fallen from a cobbler's bench. Vidar kicked his foot up and, with it, was able to still Fenrir's mouth from clamping down around him. Because of this, he was able to slit Fenrir's throat.

While this fight was being fought, all around Vidar and Fenrir death was happening. Loki was slain. The fighter who bore the flaming sword killed Freya, and the sea-serpent made a fateful end of the lightning-god Thor.

As god killed gods and all that had been created was ravished, everything would fall into the rising sea and all would become nothingness.

Chaos was restored. All was gone. Peace and darkness were restored to the backdrop of everything, the stillness in which all had been born: the quiet absence of a new Ginnungagap.

The Beginning

"It was Time's morning, When there nothing was; Nor sand, nor sea,

Nor cooling billows. Earth there was not,

Nor heaven above. The Ginnungagap was, But grass nowhere."

"The Prose Edda," by Snorri Sturluson

Before there was anything, there were fire and ice.

The abyss of nothing in which they existed was known as Ginnungagap. It was a perfect void; a vacuum, consisting solely of silence and darkness. Into this came Muspelheim and Niflheim; elemental fire, and elemental ice.

The two forces, being opposites, immediately attracted each other. The licking flames of Muspelheim reached for the cool air of Niflheim, and the bristling frost of Niflheim crept curiously to the warm shores of Muspelheim. The Ginnungagap was the chaotic realm between these extremes, and by all accounts was not a very pleasant place to be in. Opposites, even attractive ones, can never coexist nicely; so wherever the heat of Muspelheim and the chill of Niflheim came together, immediately there was trouble.

On the day everything was created, when the fire and the ice came together, instead of sparking and fizzing into the void, fire melted ice, and the ice became water. Those first few drops of water became known as Ymir; the very first being to be born in Norse tradition. His name means "The Screamer", and it is not hard to imagine why; finding yourself born in the midst of chaos and darkness, surrounded by elemental fire and ice, is bound to be frightening.

Muspelheim continued to burn at Niflheim; Niflheim continued to thaw, and of the drops of water that continued to flow was born Audhumla, a cow.

Audhumla sustained herself in the fragile, new world by licking salt off the icy plains of Niflheim. She in turn produced milk and a soft shoulder for Ymir to lean on as he grew into the first of the giants. Audhumla soon found the second; as she licked at the salty ice, she uncovered a nose and then a chin. Buried underneath Niflheim was Buri, the second giant after Ymir. Audhumla soon freed him from the salt, and he emerged to become the very first of the Aesir tribe of the gods--the more popular tribe; most of the gods the Norse people sing about were of this tribe, although there was another, the Vanir, who we shall discuss as well.

Buri begot of himself a son, whom he named Bor; "Son." As they were the first to exist and therefore the first to use language, they were able to use simple names like this, which also accounts for the name of the woman Bor later married: Bestla, which scholars post likely means "Wife." Language was quite a new thing, with all of the main players at this stage of the game still trying to figure it out. However, it is thought that the naming of words--discrete packages of energy coming from the very first word, which was a scream emanating from the mouth of the Screamer, Ymir, at the occasion of his birth--were also creative acts. These first gods were weaving the created world from the chaos they had known, just as they sang their meanings into common parlance.

Bestla was the daughter of another giant born from the same chaos which had produced Ymir and Buri. Bor and Bestla had three children: Odin, the future king of the gods and master of Valhalla, and his twin brothers, Vili and Ve.

Before Odin, the world such as it was, had existed in relative (if alternately chilly and boiling) harmony. Odin set about fixing that by plotting with his brothers to kill Ymir, which they immediately did. The three of them then set up the world as they liked, building earth as we know it from his godly corpse. From his blood flowed the oceans; his muscles and skins became the soil, and the hair growing in his skin transformed quite naturally into all of the trees and plants which crawl over the world. His brains floated up to become clouds, and the yawning arc of Ymir's skull was set above the earth and became the dome of the sky.

Odin, Vili, and Ve decided that their newly formed world needed some organization to it, so they asked four dwarves to run as fast and as far as they could in four equally opposing directions. These dwarves were different from the ones many of us are familiar with. Dwarves in the Old Nordic way were underground creatures, who were either completely made of shadows or completely invisible, although in some cases they have been described as mimicking human corpses for safety purposes. They were immensely skilled craftsmen, and most of the powerful artifacts which dot the annals and archives of Nordic legend were dwarf-made. As they are invisible, we still aren't entirely sure how they felt about this.

When the four dwarves completed Odin's instruction and arrived at the ends of the world, they picked up Ymir's skull, stabilizing the sky. They represent the four cardinal directions: North, South, East, and West; and they are the reason the sky is still standing to this very day.

Book 3: <u>Ancient Mythology</u>

<u>The Realms of the Gods Around the World</u>

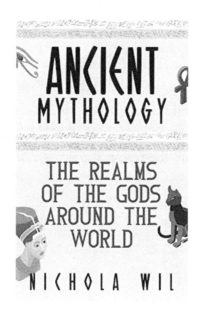

The Creation of the World

Apollo, sacred guard of earth's true core, Whence first came frenzied, wild prophetic word...

- Cicero

Ancient Greek creation myths explain how the current state of their world came to be. Given that there weren't a lot of 'people' around, it is natural that there is a lot of incest in these stories. Creation myths begin from the vast emptiness of the universe and explain the existence of the Gods.

From Chaos to Mortals

In the beginning, there was only Chaos. Chaos is described as a formless being or a place in equal measure and is female, so functions as both a void and as an unfathomable space. Chaos has feelings and is as a protector as well. In order to describe her many functions, writers always refer back to the fact that she is unfathomable.

Next sprang Gaea, Eros, and Tartarus. It is speculated in some texts that these three were the children of Chaos but as such, the particulars of their births are not described (Greekmythology.com, 2019). They simply come into existence one day. Gaea represents the Earth, Tartarus the underworld (different from Hades as described earlier), and Eros represents love. These three are the first Gods in Greek mythology.

Thanks to the influence of Eros, Gaea and Chaos were able to procreate and soon Chaos gave birth to Erebus and Nyx (darkness and night). Erebus and Nyx, in turn, had offspring named Aether (the upper air) and Hemera (day). Later, Nyx managed to fashion a series of offspring all by herself.

These offspring were many in number and are thought of as forces. Among these are:

- Moros (fate)
- Ker (doom)
- Thanatos (death)
- Hypnos (sleep)
- Oneiroi (dreams)
- Geras (old age)
- Oizus (pain)

- Nemesis (revenge)
- Eris (suffering)
- Apate (deceit)
- Philotes (sexual pleasure)
- Momos (blame)

While all of this was going on, Gaea managed to conceive Uranus.

Uranus and Cronus

Uranus is the sky and the universe and, once born, he proceeded to envelop Gaea and eventually marry her. The had three sets of children: the three cyclops (who were one-eyed giants); the Hecatoncheires, who had three hundred hands; and the twelve Titans whom you've been introduced to earlier (Greekmythology.com, 2019).

For whatever reason, Uranus was a horrible husband and father and proceeded to imprison his children within Gaea. The Earth is considered Gaea's womb and this imprisonment caused her a lot of pain. Sick of Uranus' maltreatment of her and her children, she incited her sons to kill their father. To do this, she even fashioned a sickle to make the task easier.

None of her sons except Cronus took up the challenge. Cronus and Gaea set up an ambush for Uranus one day and, as Gaea and Uranus prepared to sleep together, Cronus wielded the sickle and severed Uranus's genitals from his body. Cronus cast his father's genitals into the ocean and from the sea foam that arose when they hit the water, rose Aphrodite.

The blood that resulted from the castration led to the creation of the giants, the tree nymphs, and the Furies. What Uranus did after this is not known. He either left Earth, died, or worst of all, retired to Italy (Greekmythology.com, 2019). Cronus proceeded to assume Uranus's position as the lord of everything and turned into an even worse version of his father.

He first imprisoned the cyclops and the Hecatoncheires in Tartarus. He then married his Titan sister Rhea and proceeded to get her pregnant. One this was done though, he received a prophecy that one of his sons would kill him. Thanks to this piece of information, he proceeded to eat all of his children. Distressed, Rhea did what Gaea did and planned to kill Cronus.

She smuggled her son Zeus onto Earth where he grew up to be the man he was supposed to become and poisoned Cronus, which caused him to vomit Zeus's remaining siblings Hades, Hera, Demeter, Hestia, and Poseidon. Zeus was duly named the leader of the bunch and prepared for an all-out war against Cronus.

The Titanomachy

The next decade saw a furious battle between the Gods and the Titans. Although Cronus was too old to defend himself, his Titan siblings were equally concerned about the rise of the Gods and fought by his side. A vicious seesaw battle took place, which saw both sides close to both defeat and victory.

Gaea, who was thoroughly tired of the cruelty of first Uranus and now Cronus, supported Zeus and helped him receive his signature thunderbolt, which he is often depicted with. In addition to this, Poseidon received a trident and Hades an invisibility helmet (Greekmythology.com, 2019). This turned the tables in the war and, ultimately, with the help of the Titan Prometheus, Cronus was defeated and was exiled to Tartarus.

The Gods claimed Olympus as their own and all the Titans joined Cronus in Tartarus. Atlas, being the commander of the Titan forces, was made an example of and forced to carry the universe on his shoulders until Hercules freed him. Gaea was outraged by the exile of her children and would later conjure Typhon, a fearsome creature, to defeat Zeus. However, Typhon was defeated and the era of the Gods truly began.

Mortals

With all of creation at their disposal and with lots having been drawn to decide who got what, the Gods had nothing left to do. They thus decided to create mortal men and instructed Prometheus and Epimetheus to provide these mortals with gifts so that they could use them and, in turn, amuse the Gods by providing them entertainment.

Epimetheus who subscribed to Zeus' school of thought gave agility, speed, looks, and strength in varying proportions to mankind but left them defenseless. Prometheus, who was far kinder, realized that mankind deserved better and thus bestowed better gifts. He stole reason from Athena, fire from Hephaestus, and shared all of his knowledge with human beings.

Outraged at this, Zeus punished Prometheus by chaining him to a rock and having an eagle eat his liver every day. His liver would regrow overnight and Prometheus would thus suffer for eternity. And thus, began the dance between Gods and men, with the former treating the latter as playthings.

The Trojan War

Being a hero doesn't mean you're invincible. It just means that you're brave enough to stand up and do what's needed

. - Rick Riordan

No account of Greek mythology is complete with describing the Iliad. The Iliad is an epic by the poet Homer. Although it is set over a few weeks towards the end of the war, it first moves back in time and describes the events that led to the war and then flips forward by describing the events that are prophesied.

The Iliad is paired with the Odyssey, which is the stories of the adventures of Odysseus, king of Ithaca, on his return home from Troy. While Odysseus encounters many mythical creatures on his way back and uses his cunning to outwit them, it is the Iliad that offers multiple instances of the Gods interfering and adhering to the theme of the creation myth that humans were put on Earth to entertain the Gods.

Helen of Troy

At the center of the Iliad is the beautiful Helen. Don't get the wrong impression; Helen is merely an object throughout the book and, indeed, throughout her life. Famed for her beauty, her life is one attempted 'seduction' after another. Her birth was the result of Zeus seducing her mother, Leda, as a swan. Although the logistics of that aren't clear, the event is described in a famous poem by W.B Yeats (Greekmythology.com, 2019).

Our old friend Theseus abducted her at one point but Helen was duly returned to Sparta by her brothers Castor and Pollux. She had no trouble finding suitors for her hand and in a contest, it was Menelaus who prevailed. Given Helen's history, Menelaus had the foresight to insist on support from the remaining suitors in case of an abduction.

Paris

Meanwhile on Olympus, a party was raging and one of the guests happened to be the Trojan prince Paris. Paris was asked by Zeus to judge who was the most beautiful Goddess of them all. The contest came down to Hera, Aphrodite, and Athena. Each Goddess promised Paris a gift in return for choosing them and, ultimately, Paris chose Aphrodite who promised him the most beautiful woman in the world. Hera, with her typical maturity, decided to hate Trojans forever from that point on, which is significant for what was to follow. Helen, meanwhile unaware of being bartered against, found herself in the company of Paris. Once Menelaus discovered his trophy had been stolen, all hell broke loose.

Menelaus' brother Agamemnon, who also happened to be married to Helen's sister Clytemnestra, was the first to offend the Gods. He inadvertently killed a sacred deer, and Artemis, the God of the winds, was offended. Since wind was a prerequisite to sailing over to Troy and slaughtering everyone, a sacrifice was required. Agamemnon promptly sacrificed his daughter Iphigenia and everyone was happy (except Clytemnestra).

Paris meanwhile had raised the alarm bells in Troy and the Trojans began preparing for war. On the Greek side were a number of heroes but none mightier than Achilles after whom your tendon is named. Apparently this was the only place on his body where he could be wounded. Legend states that this was so because his mother Thetis gripped him by his ankle when dipping his body into the river Styx to grant him immortality (Greekmythology.com, 2019).

On the Trojan side is the non tendon named Hector, who was an equal to Achilles. What Troy and Hector, along with his father, the king Priam, thought of Helen is unknown. Either way, they prepared for the fight of their lives.

Family Drama

Meanwhile on Olympus, the Gods watched all of this as one might view a drama on TV. They aligned themselves on one side or the other with Zeus remaining neutral. The Gods saw the war as an opportunity to one up their siblings and did so repeatedly. For example, Aphrodite saves Paris in a one-on-one duel with Menelaus, which would have certainly killed him and ended the war. She promptly whisks him into his bedroom where Helen lays (naturally) waiting to satisfy him.

Athena urges a Trojan soldier to fire on Menelaus, which breaks the truce between the two sides and resumes the war. Apollo invokes a plague on the Greek forces and this causes a rupture between Agamemnon and Achilles. All in all, the Gods intervened in every odd manner way to change the course of the war. The actions of mortal beings are of no consequence in the end.

The duel between Achilles and Hector, which is one of the centerpieces of the book, is manipulated by Hephaestus and results in Hector's death and starts the endgame for the Trojans. Despite this, the war is ultimately decided by the famed Trojan horse. At the end of the war, everyone is dead and nothing much matters. Helen is slated to be killed by Menelaus but disrobes and is saved. In other accounts, she escapes and is never heard from again or she heads into Hades and remains with Achilles (though this is written by someone who is an Achilles fan) (Greekmythology.com, 2019).

Aftermath

Once the war ends, Agamemnon returns to find Clytemnestra ready to avenge the murder of her daughter. In the end, perhaps she is the only one who has a happy ending, seeing as everyone else died or didn't really matter too much. Odysseus roams the world on a never-ending journey until Athena intervenes and points out Ithaca to him (Greekmythology.com, 2019).

Due to events being what they are, Odysseus enrages the citizens of Ithaca, having involved the kingdom in a pointless war and having been responsible for the death of two generations of men in Ithaca. Athena again intervenes and a truce is struck, thus bringing peace to Ithaca once again.

Meanwhile, not all of the Trojans died. Aeneas, main lieutenant to Hector, managed to survive with a small band of Trojans thanks to the protection of Aphrodite (his mother), Apollo, and even Poseidon who favored the Greeks. Aeneas is mentioned more often in Roman epics because he would settle in Italy and his descendants, Romulus and Remus, would found Rome (with some help from a wolf).

This brings to a close our look at Ancient Greek mythology. As you can see, there is a lot to chronicle and a single book, let alone a single section, can hardly do justice to it. I hope this serves as a good point for you to dive into any of the stories that interest you in particular.

Now, let us leave Greece behind and travel to Sumer.

Bibliography

Kershaw, Ian. Hitler: A Biography, London: Penguin Books, 2009. Print

Kershaw, Ian. Hitler: 1889-1936 Hubris, London: Penguin Books, 1998. Print

Kershaw, Ian. Hitler: 1936-1945 Nemesis, London: Penguin Books, 2000. Print

Bullock, Alan. Hitler: A Study in Tyranny, New York: Harper & Row Publishers, 1964. Print

Ullrich, Volker. Hitler: Ascent 1889-1939, Deckle Edge, 2016

Toland, John. Adolf Hitler, The Definitive Biography, 1991.

Made in the USA
Coppell, TX
07 January 2021